my son, my son

is the author of three novels, *The Rising Sun*, *A Winter in China*, and *King Henry*. He lives in Scotland.

ALSO BY DOUGLAS GALBRAITH

The Rising Sun
A Winter in China
King Henry
Crichton

DOUGLAS GALBRAITH

my son, my son

Printed in Great Britain by Clays Ltd, St Ives plc

VINTAGE BOOKS
London

Published by Vintage 2013

2 4 6 8 10 9 7 5 3 1

Copyright © Douglas Galbraith 2012

Douglas Galbraith has asserted his right under the Copyright, Designs
and Patents Act 1988 to be identified as the author of this work

First published in Great Britain in 2012 by
Harvill Secker

Vintage
Random House, 20 Vauxhall Bridge Road,
London SW1V 2SA

www.vintage-books.co.uk

Addresses for companies within The Random House Group Limited
can be found at: www.randomhouse.co.uk/offices.htm

The Random House Group Limited Reg. No. 954009

A CIP catalogue record for this book
is available from the British Library

ISBN 9780099552680

The Random House Group Limited supports The Forest Stewardship
Council (FSC®), the leading international forest certification
organisation. Our books carrying the FSC label are printed on FSC®
certified paper. FSC is the only forest certification scheme endorsed
by the leading environmental organisations, including Greenpeace.
Our paper procurement policy can be found at:
www.randomhouse.co.uk/environment

for まこと, and さとみ,
and the separated everywhere

Contents

1 How did it start? 1

2 Abraham and Isaac 21

3 How did it really start? 51

4 Protect and survive 81

5 Men and women 117

6 In the grown-up world 149

7 Hatred 189

8 日本 222

9 Flood 257

Postscript 278

1 *How did it start?*

Summer in Scotland, the little drama almost five years ago to the day I start writing this – these things take time. It is Fife in particular, an untypical part of a largely rough country – calm waves of land capped with a richer soil that patchworks the view with ripening crops instead of hill, moor or stubbornly improved pasture. There is something almost Kentish about it, though no hop-fields these days and not yet any vineyards under the thickening air. It is less spoiled also – less concrete, fewer people, narrower and less cluttered roads and beyond the low horizon the North Sea and a fringe of undeveloped sandy strands and coastal cliffs promising, it is said, fossils and gems to the patient hunter. Watercolourists speckle the old fishing villages, drinking in the endless supplies of terracotta, whitewash and ultramarine. Awestruck golfers come from across the world for the course they must play just once before they die. There is a picturesque university where adolescents freeze through crystalline winters as they are invited to take an interest in the Grand Unified Theory or the doomed efforts of Justinian. It is a place people choose, a good place to bring up a family.

The scene is a railway station, just a halt on the line really, a post-Beeching survival spared a few decades ago not for the more distant trainless town but for the RAF base at Leuchars, for the convenience of officers wishing to take part of their leave in the London clubs, for the more punctual keeping of

appointments in HQ or Whitehall. It was all very serious then
– the colourless graphics of the 1950s showed how the Soviet
nuclear strike force could be expected to descend from the
north-east, how life as we knew it would end if only they
could get past the interceptors. That has all long gone and the
warplanes thundering in the cloudless sky are not defending
anyone now. We are safe – it is 2003 and the maps on the
briefing room walls are of Basra and Baghdad.

The service up from London pulls away and I watch the
homecomings and the visitors being greeted. The minicabs
make off with their fares, then a bus collects its passengers
from the shelter. It is not a busy time and I am soon alone
with one other traveller. I look over the car park, searching
for a patch of dirty red which indicates our permanently
unwashed car and my wife and sons come to collect me and
make the twenty-minute journey to our home. Nothing yet,
but it doesn't matter on such a warm and luminous evening.

They were there four days ago, two boys six and four years
old, a little grumpy at being dragged out on some trip that
had nothing to do with them. They are different, though
clearly a pair with the same straight chestnut brown hair, the
same deep brown eyes and the skin by no means dark, but
not quite fair either, a skin that takes the sun easily and might
suggest, if you saw them out of context, something southern.
In another country they stand out, but in multi-ethnic
Britain – and that includes even Fife these days – they are
noticed only for themselves. Their names, if you were to
overhear them, would be a more helpful clue: the little one
with his head and face so much rounder than his brother is
Makoto, his elder brother Satomi. He was once called

something else, but even I call him Satomi now, as did all his schoolmates ten days earlier at the first, and almost certainly last, sports day I will ever attend as a parent.

It's a small country school, probably no more than twenty pupils, two teachers in a pretty stone schoolhouse not much changed or expanded since it was built for the purpose a hundred years back. It's been there long enough to name its own address – School Brae, from the top of which the fertile levels of the Howe of Fife and the worn Lomond Hills can be seen through the classroom windows, now green, now white as the year turns. The field of competition is the village recreation ground, just an acre and a half with swings and a roundabout at one end. Makoto, still a year too young to be a pupil, amuses himself on these as the action unfolds. A sportsman emerges, face grim with effort and aggression as he gets his chest increasingly covered with gold stickers – never enough, it seems; one to watch for the future. Satomi is happier with his honourable collection of silver and bronze, perhaps having inherited his father's disdain for winning The final event is a longer race around the perimeter. Satomi falls back, flopping with exhaustion, but delighted all the same as he runs towards me and breathlessly declares 'I ran faster than somebody'.

Already self-contained at four years old, Makoto has paid no attention at all to the proceedings. Besides myself the other particular observer of Satomi's efforts has been his mother. Expressionless, determinedly apart, this small Japanese woman, Tomoko by name, looks on frigidly and with mounting anxiety as she watches her son, so visibly different from her, interact with western teachers and western children and all in a western language. Though no rational investigator could find any evidence for it, she is sure in her own mind that everyone else there is part of a conspiracy to loosen her grip on her children. No one would suspect she has any connection with me. Indeed, she is clearly concerned not to have any connection. All afternoon she will not look at me or speak a single word, even to explain why she is not speaking. This is not unusual. The behaviour neither surprises me nor, at this late stage in a long decline, embarrasses me. We look like a couple who have had a row that morning, although in truth there has been an openly declared and exhausting war for the last five years. On this occasion there is something different about it, something of the extremist in her insistence that I do not exist, that her children's father is simply not there, not to be thought of. It was a necessity, I suppose, given what she had planned. The signs were there, clear in retrospect, but in those days there were still things I didn't believe people were capable of and I couldn't read them correctly. I was outclassed in deception. With some regret, I know that will never happen again.

Sports day is over and it's time to go. The red car — the one I am waiting for a fortnight later at the station — is parked by the side of the road with its doors open, Makoto already strapped into his seat in the back. The goodbyes are made, his elder brother's foreign name chorused by a dozen childish Scottish voices. What did they make of such a strange word? Nothing, it seems now as I search my memory for details, nothing at all. They pronounced it confidently, thoughtlessly — any pleasant word would do for a name, none was worth fighting over or meant anything other than the person who bore it. That's Primary One for you – all the damage of life not yet done.

I think back on this as I pace the platform and check my watch. The other traveller is still there, the only other person now. I glare at the public telephone, but she is standing too close to it and would overhear. I radiate a desire for her to move away but she insensitively drifts a step closer. Cars emerge from a bend in the road and run along a short straight past the station before disappearing amongst the outlying houses of Leuchars. Traffic is light now and I can hear individual engines approaching before I can see anything. I stare at that point where they first become visible, willing the next one to be red. Sometimes it is, though not the one I'm waiting for. I've been away four days and I want to see my boys.

'See you Thursday,' Tomoko said to me the previous Sunday as I got the train down. She was not always convincing, but was at her best that day: completely natural, which can't have been easy.

I was looking forward to getting away and felt no guilt about it, though I would later. As a writer my workplace was a room in the house with the latest drawing of a train being pushed under the door by Satomi, or Makoto walking in whenever he liked to pull all the books off the shelf until he found Livy's *War with Hannibal* – not out of precocious genius but on account of the fascinating picture of a lion on the cover. I made desultory efforts to defend this space, but they were never wholehearted – the child always being more interesting than the work. I lived with my children very nearly every day of their early lives and skipped all the articles in the Sunday newspapers about work–life balance or workaholic absentee fathers as having nothing to do with me. In the adult household this constant mutual presence was perhaps not such a good thing. The opportunities for periodic escape offered by more conventional careers, the relieving and low-risk infidelities of the sales conference or team-building weekend have no doubt saved more marriages than any of us will ever admit. These are not a feature of the writing life, which has to fall back for its Bunburying on the self-declared 'research trip' and it was in this light that I saw my journey to London: necessary, but also welcome. Whether excessive contact with the mother of my children hastened the end or delayed it is difficult to say; it was, after all, just such a rare period of absence that she was waiting for.

What do I recall of a short trip to London in the summer of 2003? I find, as I come to write this, that much is already vague or lost. What did I read on the train on the way down? I can't say now – something enjoyable to add to the holiday mood, or did I pose with a sternly intellectual work-related tome like *Documents on the Rape of Nanking* or Auden and Isherwood's self-absorbed *Journey to a War*? I do remember why I was going: to fulfil my part of a publishing contract for two novels, to earn a living, to provide. More specifically to root around in the Newspaper Library at Colindale on the trail of the fears and desires of western expatriates in China in 1937, the stage for my story.

The details have gone again – nothing remains from getting in to the cheap hotel just off the Bayswater Road, or the rest of that first night away in the warm London summer, a foreign climate for me. Then, next morning, breakfast in a café somewhere or on the move as I head down into the Tube and change lines to turn north and the long run through an unfamiliar townscape. I'm recognisable as the outsider; too interested in the novelties passing by and constantly checking that I haven't managed to get myself lost yet. Hampstead, Golders Green, Hendon Central. I get out at the next stop and find the place with unaccustomed ease. I'm an old hand at libraries. Too old, I think sometimes and they give me an ambiguous feeling now – partly of confidence at knowing the ropes, partly of doubt, of failure at still being there at all when so many of the readers I knew have moved on to what seem to me, in my ignorance, more concrete lives. Apart from the staff they are disturbingly peopled; largely by the young going through the hoops of a tertiary education from which they are sure to move on soon, and then at the other end the living warnings who always fill me with dread. I've never known a research library without at least one super-articulate tramp, the sort of character one imagines was treated unjustly in a fellowship election in the late 1950s and has struggled ever since to regain his equilibrium. They come in for warmth in winter and sit as motionless as the furniture before suddenly coming to life and growling alarmingly at the name of an old enemy honourably cited in the latest journals. I edge away, but then catch my own face in the glass of a dusty cabinet and am hit by that surge of fear – the same as last time, only worse.

I convince the librarians of my good faith (not always easy) and settle in to the cinematic dark of the microfilm reading room. The pages of the *China Press* for late 1937 stream by and I begin to pick out the novelist's raw material; all the most highly coloured and poignant and pregnant ephemera the historians so reliably leave out. Seventy years ago is an interesting time — at once distant and near; part history, but for others very definitely living memory. I peer into the world when my parents were small children, the age my own children are now. The events recorded are as distant and strange for me as the Iraq War or the attack on the World Trade Center towers will be for them, idling through a history book or watching a documentary some time in the 2070s. The period dress, the outmoded vehicles, the distinctively inferior picture quality of early digital video will all mark it as remote until they recall with a start 'I was four then; that's my era too, or just about. I can almost remember it.'

The trick of the novelist is not to be learned about his material, but to cultivate in himself the illusion that what he knows is truly a memory; that he did not read it, but recalls it from having been there, just there where I can recognise myself in the crowd — that man in the trilby and the white shirt with the wide collar. I was a better dresser in the thirties. I become the one who looks up and then runs for the shelter as he hears the air-raid siren, the one who bought a Shanghai corporation lottery ticket from the kiosk that morning and sat through the matinée at the Grand, staying for the Paramount newsreel and even for the Popeye cartoon at the end, though he never found it funny.

North London recedes and the western enclaves of Shanghai in the late 1930s take over. I drink a cocktail in the Metropole Garden — Don José and his orchestra entertaining — and catch up on the news. The Sino-Japanese War has moved inland. It's happening elsewhere now but civilians are still being bombed from the air; not out of malice particularly, but rather a sincere inability to hit the right target while pursuing one's ideals. For all the Chinese propaganda – 400 NIPPONESE PLANES DOWNED says one column – it's a one-sided affair. Japan is the killer; my wife's people, and to a lesser extent my children's people too. I peer closely and refocus the projected newsprint as I make another note. I am not much troubled by the thought, believing that these connections, if they exist at all, cannot be dangerous over such distance and time. I have built my life on the assumption that ties of this sort can be broken or easily superseded by others more intimate, reasonable and humane. In the quiet whirr of cooling fans and the heat of projector lamps I spectate on the suffering once caused by clashing identities and even now do not expect to become personally involved.

In the edition for 4 September 1937 I find an interesting byway of history, deception and the heart. It concerns the one truly great image of the Sino-Japanese War, a photograph that only needs to be seen once to be always remembered. It shows a sturdy baby boy alone in the ruins of South Station, Shanghai moments after it had been bombed by the Empire of Japan. It is one of the images of the century, recognised by many even when they do not know exactly what it shows. The child is tonsured in the local manner, conspicuously well fed and even shod with sandals, though he can hardly have started to walk. Every detail speaks of his parents' care for him, but now his white shirt, clean that morning, is dark with blood. He sits up straight, mouth open – this is a photograph you can hear – and cries with all his strength. In the background there is a litter of corrugated iron panels blasted from the station roof in the same storm of shrapnel and

debris that has nearly killed him. Most disturbing is the child's
solitude, his apparent helplessness. This is what gives the
image its power to move, what prompted the description for a
recent usage of the picture: 'The Last Creature Alive in South
Station, Shanghai'. It is also completely untrue. Look to the
left where now you see only blank paper shading towards the
edge of the book. Is it in any way questionable? Does it arouse
the slightest suspicion that you might have been misled?
Probably not – in some ways we are all too trusting.

The picture in its famous – inevitably one must say in its
iconic – form is in fact an artfully selected single frame taken
by H. S. 'Newsreel' Wong, first on the scene for Metrotone
News. What has been cut out from the left-most third of this
scene, either by Wong's choice of composition or by a picture
editor later cropping it, is the boy's father and his elder brother,

about six years old, holding himself erect and still as he looks directly at the camera from where he stands by the tracks. He has just been put there by his father who at this very moment, this 1/30th of a second, is in the act of moving back into the picture to put his hands under the arms of his infant, pick him up and take both his children home. For all we know the South Station baby, at the age of seventy-five or six, is still alive and well. The suggested caption of the *China Press* for the fuller picture was 'A father trying to help his two badly shocked and injured children'. This version was distributed at the time, and yet it never took root, the 'abandoned' South Station baby remaining the preferred form to this day. It has stayed that way because it makes a more powerful appeal, though to what exactly is a dark question. If one assumes the best of intentions – that it was an editorial decision to create a more powerful anti-war image – the affair has ended ironically. The manipulated history of the picture is now best known among the wilder fringes of modern Japanese nationalism. Here it has a new purpose, not to say that the baby was never abandoned, but rather that, as a 'fake' image, it should lead us to doubt that he was ever bombed, that his shirt was ever soaked in blood, that he was ever in pain or fear; to doubt even that much of the Sino-Japanese War ever happened at all.

Hunger and growing eye-strain call me back to London in 2003. I flick the switch to turn the reader off and head out for lunch. There was a café just across the road, perhaps right by the underground station, and I think it was here in this marginal, resigned place that I took a break three days in a row; three cups of coffee and, presumably, something to eat. Though I haven't checked and would not be surprised if it is wrong, my memory of the view from the window always shows me an overcast and sometimes rainy scene. I can recover nothing else from those three hours but think it likely, because it is such a strong habit of mine, that I bought and read a newspaper each day. Pursuing this clue I find myself five years later in another library at the other end of the country, trying to do for myself what I usually do for historical and semi-fictional characters: recovering a recent, but already partly lost history. What was the news in late June and early July 2003? I wind through another coil of microfilm and find that my expectations have become wildly prejudiced against the facts. The banning of fox hunting, a Green Paper on civil partnerships, and the death of Katharine Hepburn were the leading talking points of the day. Violence in Iraq and Afghanistan is there, but less prominently than I assumed. It was the early, relatively quiet days of the occupation – the coming insurgency not yet in gear, optimism still just about possible without seeming a fool or an obvious propagandist. One reason for forgetting whatever it was I read over those three lunchtimes is the visual dullness of modern newspapers when compared to what I had seen in the archive. Today there is a more strict graphical self-censorship by which written reports of death – 'Imam and nine others killed at mosque' – are illustrated by a photograph of the living and uninjured framed by a half-demolished wall as if this might convey the reality of warfare while at the same time maintaining an all-important decency.

Later, at the hotel, lethargically looking on from the bed, I know it must have been the same on the television news, a coy sluicing of dilute blood from the steps, voiced over with that sinister and rarely challenged excuse that the rest is too distressing to broadcast. It's the family viewing version of history — values confused, truthfulness half-hearted at best and, for what it's worth, with no ambition to add to our stock of great images.

*

My routine for the trip is established and the work is going well. These days I think of visits to libraries and archives as a sort of raid — a typical fantasy metaphor for those leading unacceptably inactive lives — get in, get what you want, get out and away before that dead air penetrates too deeply into the lungs. I've heard that modern zookeepers stimulate their more thoughtful charges by placing food in hard to get places and I wonder if librarians might make a small dent in the joylessness of writers and academics by placing obstacles in their way: a booby trap here, an electrified shelf there, the odd page impregnated with deadly poison. There would be casualties of course, but perhaps not so many as to outweigh the general elevation of spirits, the happy bragging later in the pub of how one cheated death during the recent consultation of an encyclopaedia, the sweet solemnity of mourning fallen comrades.

I will, no doubt, have considered the telephone in the hotel room squatting on the melamine chipboard side table by the box of lilac tissues and the tourist leaflets. Call home? The parent's taste for freedom never lasts more than a few hours, or days at most before we're missing them again. What have my boys been up to? It would mean talking to my wife — not easy, perhaps not even possible. The mere thought deters me and I make no calls at any time from London, settling instead for looking forward to that Thursday evening when I'll step off the train and be with them again in the flesh.

This pattern is broken one evening by the coincidental presence in London of an old friend. We arrange to meet and spend some of our time at the Globe Theatre on the South Bank. On the stage a disaster unfolds, one so total and unredeemed that by the end of the evening the critics have been drawn into an inappropriate relationship with the production — namely, one of pity. The next day, flinching from its concentrated awfulness they comment generously on how rare it is to be able to see a staging of Christopher Marlowe's *Dido, Queen of Carthage* and note the quality of the incidental music. Two lessons are delivered at once: if a theatrical piece is still so rare after several centuries it is rare for a reason, and if the incidental music is offered as a reason for going, on no account go. The groundlings, a few busloads of foreign students, are still too young and uncertain of what they deserve to do anything other than feign appreciation. No doubt the language barrier saved them from the worst — wax in the ears of these new Odyssean travellers. In just the same way, I suppose, that it would save me from the pain of enduring an evening of below-par kabuki at the Minami-za. This is a very contemporary production, that is to say one in which the director nakedly yearns for authorship and brings an abundance of his own ideas to the text. In this case it's worth a try as the text isn't up to much; not a play at all really, just a cut and pasted undergraduate translation of an epic, but not especially dramatic Roman poem. The gods manipulate mortals who, dressed as children in a playground setting, manipulate the only thing too defenceless to stand up to them, a real human child, though played in this instance by a plastic doll moved around the stage by some character I never quite got the hang of. It isn't working, and the mixed expressions of panic and anger in the actors' eyes tell me I'm not the only one to have noticed this. With a long hour to go I drift off and look up at the circle of blue above the Globe's open courtyard. I watch airliners cut across it, unconcerned about who might be in them or where they are going. Perhaps I should think better of the play now, give it some credit for the durable wisdom of those old themes – that blindness is universal, the condition varying only in degree, that we never see what touches most intimately on our fortunes until it is too late.

It ends. There is a kindly excess of applause while my friend and I bolt for the doors. What then? I can plausibly reconstruct a few beers, the pleasure of finding ourselves in agreement on the latest news as we proceed smoothly to diagnosis, prescription and a better, though imaginary world. We are sunk deep in the heart of the Iraq lie with the occupation forces still hotfoot in pursuit of the non-existent doomsday machines that have justified it all. I look back on those days as one of the three diverse episodes in my life (and perhaps in the life of any stay-at-home Briton born in 1965) that gave me some insight into what it is to live in a totalitarian society where the pretended belief in untruths has become mandatory. The first was the Falklands War and the middle chapter came with the sense of being bullied into a moronic consensus on the death of the Princess of Wales — a kitsch drama managed to no small extent by the same impresarios at work in 2003. The Iraq adventure is already going wrong, but the best newspapers are still printing articles hailing the victims' liberation and anticipating fearful discoveries any day. My friend and I share astonishment at the flagrancy of these lies, at the submissive idiocy of believing them. We agree that we could not be so easily fooled. Just a little theatrically I look over my shoulder — is it safe to say these things?

Around closing time there is the sense — maudlin, laughable, obviously drink-fuelled — that if we of our generation, not as individuals you understand but our sort, had been the ones to seek power rather than to shrink from it in disgust, much suffering could have been avoided. That philosophers make reluctant kings — so rarely make kings of any sort — is one of the most regular patterns of human affairs. From this there arises in the world-weary mind a concern that the greatest episodes of human destruction occur not by mischance, but through a mechanism that reliably guides the most inadequate to those positions from which they can do most harm. They may have nothing to recommend their candidacy, but still the way opens before them. Where does the fault lie? Surely it is only partly in the fact that the levers of power are none too clean, and partly in the hygienic prissiness of all the better types who keep their distance: the commentators, the academics, the journalists, the social novelists, all the sterilely articulate who make a career out of implying how much better the world would have been if only they hadn't stood by and done nothing.

What does all that mean? It means it's closing time. My friend and I part.

'Too bad about the play.'

I make my way westward across the hot dark city, rattling in the Tube, emerging at Marble Arch to amble down the Bayswater Road. I'm trying to follow the thread of these thoughts convinced, as one is after the requisite number of beers, that I'm on the trail of something worthwhile. But I'm too tired and it's too late and I am relieved in any case from making any further efforts by the appearance of a large fox. It is about three metres away, just behind the railings of Hyde Park. The ground is elevated above the pavement so we find ourselves precisely eye to eye. I move towards it a few inches in what I imagine to be an unthreatening manner, and then a few inches more. The fox does not retreat but continues to stare at me and there we remain, fixed for half a minute until it loses interest, turns slowly away and lopes out of sight. Someone, I suppose, would write a poem about it – but I just go to bed.

I slip back into the thirties for one last day at the newspaper library; the hostess bars, the mediums and fortune-tellers advertising in the classifieds, the price of an Empire Flying Boat ticket to Penang, an announcement that the Tokyo Olympics would definitely go ahead in 1940, the bombing raids, the refugees, the lies. I pack up at the end of the day and am left with one last image of the place. From behind me comes a rapid skittering sound and an exclamation. At last someone has stumbled on the joke microfilm reader – there's one in every library, placed there by bored librarians in search of entertainment. This one has been cunningly rigged to

unravel the film in the wrong direction and to operate at only
two speeds; zero, and super-turbo. I give the chap a bit of time
to sort himself out, but when I turn round I find that he is still
deeply enmeshed in his own Norman Wisdom moment – a
hapless Laocoön of the thinking life, embarrassed at being
brought low by thirty metres of celluloid serpent. His problem
seems all the worse for being witnessed by me. I give him an
encouraging smile and slip out.

*

And so the train back north, alone on the platform at Leuchars
station with the jets still thundering overhead. I have already
dialled my home number once from the public telephone and
now dial again and listen to it ring and ring. They must be on
their way, then – just a confusion about the times. I think
back to our parting the previous Sunday. Could there have
been any misunderstanding? The right day was clearly
mentioned, followed by a needling 'have fun'. I construct
reassuring scenarios but cannot stop the fear rising. There are
other possibilities, possibilities that have threatened in the
past, that have had certain, perhaps inadequate, precautions
taken against them. They are possibilities that have also been
suppressed, shied away from, cheaply bargained with for
another year of peace. Humanity's talent for living in a double
reality explains a lot that would otherwise seem strange –
why we don't save ourselves, why we build cities at the foot of
volcanoes, even when we don't have to.

I abandon the wait and start making my way home by
public transport. This involves two buses and then a taxi ride

of four or five miles. It cannot be much before ten o'clock when I arrive. The house has not burned down, it is not surrounded by police cars. Although it is still light, it is also past the children's bedtime and so I notice that all the curtains are open. The red car stands on the driveway. The garage door is open. The doors of the house are locked and I have no key. I become very conscious of the possibility of being observed from the other houses which curve around ours in a tight cul de sac, so I move through a side gate into the back garden. There I pace for a long time, partly working over the problem of how to break into my own house, but mostly struggling with the fear of what I might find inside. In truth it is not the prospect of finding Tomoko's small, manipulative corpse that bothers me. It is the other thing — that extreme and unspeakable news story one sees once or twice a year, blowing in sensationally from a far-off country, always impossible to understand. Something makes me believe she is capable of it and that's why I don't want to know what's in my house.

I get a screwdriver from the garage. My breath is short and my hands trembling as I lever open a window and climb in. The place is very silent and I stand still for several minutes before being able to make any decision. There are eight principal rooms. That's seven others to enter — seven thresholds, seven doors to be opened. Very slowly I go round them all, hesitating before entering each one. On the way I notice that an item of furniture is missing. Books have gone from the shelves and where there were two prints hanging together on the wall there is now only one. I go upstairs to the bedrooms. Everything is neat and empty. I come to the closed door of the master bedroom, the appropriate setting for horrors and tragedies. Inside there is nothing worse than two pairs of pyjamas lying in the middle of the floor in vaguely child-shaped heaps. They have my boys' fresh smell and my hallucinating skin detects a warmth that can no longer be real.

Downstairs I notice a single letter on the doormat. It is from the Royal Mail and is addressed to Tomoko. It was not her plan that it should have been sent, let alone seen by me. It is the one imperfection of the crime scene, the lead one expects in a piece of mass-market fiction before the story really gets going. I open it and read that they are pleased to confirm her instructions for forwarding mail to her new address: Studio Shinmido, Yodogawa, Osaka, Japan.

I find myself back in the garage, though I'm not sure why – perhaps it is just to return the screwdriver. I know something of the law, I know something of Japan and Britain too, I know a great deal about Tomoko, and so I know I will never see my children again. Outside, a neighbour goes by, carrying a watering can to a flowerbed. I draw back to avoid being seen. My heart is fluttering strangely, but will not stop. I see the miniature bow and arrow I made for Satomi, the red dragon kite we flew at the beach and Makoto's tricycle. I look up and see the open rafters, the looped cable hanging from a nail.

2   *Abraham and Isaac*

When should you kill your children? The question occurs rarely to the modern parent and mostly for mundane reasons, or in the absence of reason. The cases – and there is a steady stream of them – are prized by the media and always assured of a substantial audience. We are strongly drawn to these stories, the strength of the emotions they elicit, the need for comforting expressions of collective outrage and grief, the aesthetic satisfaction of spectating on the fundamentally tragic. There's no doubt about it, from the sophisticated horror-frisson of Medea all the way down to the latest freezer baby stories from France and Germany, we all have an appetite for a good parental child-killing.

The presentation of these episodes follows a well-worn format – fathers hurting mothers after losing out in family breakdown; mothers engaging in a bit of after the fact contraception (bad), or acting while under the compulsion of a mental illness (not exactly good, but still deserving of a little compassion from the more advanced sources). Other instances, typically where the perpetrator is intellectually subnormal, are born simply of the need to have the greatest possible effect on a defenceless subject, or out of boredom, or sadism, or an inability to cope with anything very much at all. In these cases, more psychiatrically than socially interesting, the child becomes an instrument, played for a few months or even years until, during a more *forte* passage, it

breaks and the whole ghastly story comes out and metamor-
phoses cathartically into a public inquiry – the ritualism of
which requires that the words 'never again' be pronounced at
some point during the tiresomely familiar proceedings.

These and other similar varieties are secular child-killing;
our day and age's particular form ranging from simple moral
incapacity through temporary emotional imbalance to the
extremist and carefully plotted protest against the culture of
mass divorce – the only adequate expression of hatred for the
victorious partner, the only way of repossessing what one has
been intolerably dispossessed of by the family courts. In the
extensive typology of infanticide (allowing that the crime
can include some pretty grown-up infants), these forms have
one thing in common that clearly identifies them as a set: no
one approves of them. No reason is offered, however confused
or bizarre, as to why these killings might after all be acts of
virtue. It will seem odd, especially to the enlightened reader,
even to raise such an idea, but to ignore this possibility lacks
cultural breadth as well as a sense of history. It is to look away
from the fact that close to the dark heart of our moral tradition a child-killer is held up as an honourable figure and a
model for action. According to this tradition, there is a right
time to kill your child and it is good to do so. Naturally, we
rush to say these things are all in the dim and distant past,
but as we remember from our own childhoods, we must first
check under the bed before being quite sure the monster is
gone.

Abraham, for the sake of convenience, is the monster's
name; or Avraham, or Ibrahim if you prefer. Other cultures
and times have other names and other stories, but for us, for

now Abraham will do. While this alarming character still features in the *Child's First Book of Bible Stories,* that volume doesn't sell quite as well as it used to and so it might be worthwhile briefly recounting the essentials. Abraham had a special relationship with God who favoured him with numerous messages from on high. One day the message from God to Abraham was that he should take his only son Isaac to a place he would point out to him and there cut his throat and burn his corpse as an offering. Abraham was keen to obey – the Bible tells us that he rose especially early the next morning so that he could get everything organised. Once he had gathered a couple of servants together and loaded up his ass with chopped wood for the fire, he went off with Isaac to find the right place to kill him. After a few days of wandering Abraham decided that one of the hills looked suitable. He told his two servants to wait while he and his son climbed the hill to worship. He told his servants that they would both return. He loaded up the wood on Isaac's back, making his son carry the fuel for his own sacrificial pyre to the top of the hill. Abraham carried the knife himself. When Isaac asked his father about the lack of an animal to sacrifice, he was told not to worry about that – God would provide. It goes largely unnoticed that Abraham had a distinctive, if rather disturbing sense of humour. Once there, an altar was built and the wood arranged for the burnt offering. Abraham tied up his son, no doubt fearing ungodly resistance as soon as young Isaac realised that his poor old dad had lost his marbles. Abraham took his knife and was on the very point of murdering his child when – and one can only apologise for the weakness of the plotting – an angel appeared and told him not to bother because it was really the thought that counted. A ram, trapped in a nearby thicket, was slaughtered instead.

At no point in the story is there any suggestion that Abraham is not actively intent on killing his child. Indeed, that is the essential element — he would have failed the test had he not been such a willing executioner. Abraham as a child-killer, from whom Isaac has just been rescued in the nick of time, is even more beloved of the Lord than he was before. For this great virtue there is a great reward. God speaks to Abraham again and tells him: because you have done this, because you have put this voice in your head before your own child I will multiply your children and your children's children as the stars of heaven and the sand on the shore. Because you have obeyed my voice your children shall be part of all the nations of the earth. And here, precisely, is the heart of the story — that the mind of Abraham was not unique and isolated in a single time and place, but that it was a reservoir, the poisonous contents of which have flowed down through the generations and been inherited by us all.

So much for the old story. Does it still mean anything today? Could it, in this modern world? In one very direct, though rare, way it does. While Moloch- or Baal-related murders are unheard-of simply because the myths and parables of these cults are now largely unknown, the persistence of Abrahamic religions means the persistence of the story. And the persistence of the story occasionally means the persistence of the act.

On 6 January 1990 Cristos Valenti, after a period of problems with alcohol and growing psychosis, spent the day doing chores at his home in California. God had been speaking to him quite a lot over the last few months and did so again that day while he was painting the house. He required Cristos to offer him his daughter, the 'little one', as a sacrifice. As in the original version, the emotional flatness of the main actor is a notable feature. In this case, and partially to his credit, Cristos did later tell the authorities that the message nearly caused him to fall off his ladder. But it was only surprise that caused this and not doubt. In the evening he read from the Bible to his youngest child and explained the pictures to her. The other children of the household fell asleep in front of the television and then their mother, exhausted from her cleaning job, also fell asleep. Cristos left the house with his daughter and drove with her to a nearby park. They walked together to a grove of trees, that most ancient of settings for symbolic acts. There he told her to lie on the grass and recite a Christian prayer while he took out a knife and killed her. He looked up at the stars and then prayed by the body for a short while before picking it up and returning home. It was his eldest daughter, the dead girl's older sister, who answered the door. 'Call the police,' said Cristos Valenti, 'I've given her to God.'

The date is significant: Epiphany in the calendar of the killer's religion, the night the wise men saw the star that would lead them to the birthplace of Jesus. Not long before being killed by her father the girl had been in a school Nativity play, playing the role of a star. In subsequent statements to the police Valenti explained with poignant and obviously damaged simplicity, that 'God needed her, to put her in a star'. From the purely textual point of view it is clear that there has been a confusion here between Abraham and Isaac and the Nativity stories. But that, perhaps, is a side issue.

At the ensuing trial Valenti maintained the manner of a man who knew he had done the right thing. The jurors heard evidence that he was mentally ill and, notwithstanding that they largely shared his religion, tended to view his claims about messages from God as confirmation of madness. They also received an explanation from the judge that malice aforethought was required for there to be a conviction of murder in the first degree. In the serenity with which Cristos had carried out the killing, the moral self-confidence of his statements to police, and his untroubled demeanour in court it was hard to find much evidence of that. He was acquitted of murder.

One would want the case to be unique, a freakish curiosity of the criminal record of no wider significance – but it is not so. Only four years later Robert Blair, while holidaying with his wife and son in Concord, New Hampshire, conceived the notion that God wanted him to kill his son. In a later local newspaper report he specifically cited the example of Abraham and Isaac. Just as Abraham had to offer his sacrifice at an appointed place revealed to him from on high, so also for Blair it was essential that the killings (this sacrifice was to include his wife as well as his son) take place in the required location, in this instance a particular room in a Concord motel – the room in which the idea had first occurred to him. He was a patient man, and eighteen months elapsed before the family booked in again and rented the room they had stayed in before. On the afternoon of 25 March 1996 Blair walked to a nearby hardware store and bought a hammer which he hid under the bed in the room. That evening he discussed with his wife his belief that he should kill their son, showing her the hammer he intended to use. The idea was poorly received and Blair pretended to give it up, depositing the hammer in a bin outside. That night while they slept God revealed to Robert Blair that 'he would be cast into a lake of fire' if he welched on the deal. In addition, he heard the voice of an angel commanding him to go through with it. He went outside to retrieve the hammer and did what he believed he had been told to do.

Blair testified in his own defence at the trial, remarking confidently to the jury that 'in my opinion, I'm sane. I acted under the command of God. I do not suffer delusions or hallucinations . . . I was very rational . . . I understood what I did.' The jury agreed with him and convicted him on two counts of murder. Oddly, Blair was soon to repent of his declaration of sanity and launch a quixotic appeal. The grounds were, amongst others, that he was probably mad after all and that the first court had erred on a technicality by not allowing him enough time to discuss with the jury just how dangerous he really was. Unsurprisingly, the appeal did not succeed.

Here are two cases close in time and place, and no doubt a diligent researcher could find others. Even so, it's only two cases and one might ask if anything can be read into such rarities. Is the Abraham and Isaac story, from the point of view of public safety, no more than an antique version of today's Superman mythology which is said (apocryphally, for all I know) to make its own small contribution to child mortality by persuading the occasional ten-year-old to 'fly' out of a top-floor window? These casualties are distressing, but for society as a whole very slight and they would hardly justify suppressing their imaginative source. If stories have to be harmless we might end up telling very few stories at all. We could go further and say that if a story hinting at moral ambiguity when it comes to harming one's own children proves to be of interest only to a marginal minority, and actively influences the behaviour of fewer still, we might be entitled to shrug with regret but pass on in a world with bigger problems. Is this just a weirdo issue? Does it have nothing to do with ordinary people?

Happily, some pertinent and very fresh data on exactly this issue is to hand. Only a few days before I write these sentences in late January 2009 a much larger, and no doubt more representative, jury of over six hundred people considered a similar case. The defendant was Abraham himself, or more precisely the Abraham and Isaac story, its content, its meaning, whether it is to be reviled or respected, whether it could really be true that Abraham spread his child-killer genes through the whole world. The forum for this mock trial was the synagogue of California's Irvine University, the trial report an article in the local *Orange County Register*. Mr Jonathan Shapiro, prosecuting, opened with a joke: please take careful note, he advised, of the difference between the defendant and his own son, also named Abraham, sitting there in the front row and feeling rather nervous, given the subject under discussion. Laughter in court, but perhaps with a little nagging awkwardness under the surface. And what about young Abraham Shapiro? How did he feel when he discovered at the end of the day's proceedings that he lived in a society that could only convict his ancient namesake of attempted murder by a 'slim' majority; that is to say, in a society in which nearly half the adults could not publicly affirm that a parent who would try to kill their child on the instructions of an external authority was guilty of a crime? We don't know. He wasn't asked.

The *Orange County Register* raises no doubts about the mental health of these three hundred or so apologists for child sacrifice, let alone suggesting that any enquiries be made by the authorities into how they treat their own children. Perhaps it is right not to worry unduly. The conclusion to be drawn here is not that the respondents in this substantial sample of public opinion are as mad as Cristos Valenti or Robert Blair, or that they represent a threat to anyone's safety. The conclusion is altogether more disturbing — that whatever lurks beneath the surface of the Abraham and Isaac story is indeed a seed widely spread throughout humanity, that it has been planted deep in the minds of ordinary people.

In the light of the mock trial we might return with renewed uncertainty to the two real trials of Valenti and Blair. In spite of the similarity in their circumstances, one resulted in a conviction and the other in an acquittal. If the beliefs, or parental behaviours, of nearly half of the large Irvine University audience were typical then we might reasonably assume that some of the same views were to be found in the real jurors at Valenti's trial, also held in California. Reading through the facts of the case and its outcome again there is the risk of a sudden, almost violent change of perspective: the jury's decision to acquit now appears to dilute society's disapproval of a parent's lethal disposal of their own child, to be making a concession not to the formal defence of insanity, but to those attitudes that grant a parent special licence for the harm they do to their own offspring. Whatever the record says, it could be seen as a victory for the Abraham defence. We might reasonably doubt whether, if Valenti had killed someone else's child – or an adult during the same incident, as Blair did – he would still have been acquitted of murder, however deranged.

*

A European reader, or an Indian, or even a Japanese for that matter might still feel unengaged by such remote examples. Strange things are always coming out of the United States, now quite alone in the developed world in the persistence of its religiosity and its ever-fresh fascination with violence. It would be unfair, on the strength of such slender evidence, to suggest that humanity as such has a problem – it might be a local phenomenon, the rest of us, other nations, other cultures, might remain entirely innocent. What do we find elsewhere?

In Europe a post-theistic and largely post-nationalistic mindset has taken some of the heat out of child sacrifice – the voice of God, or of political or nationalistic god-equivalents doesn't seem to get through quite as viciously as it does on other continents. Reason jams it and, doubtless, saves a handful of lives every year. It's true that there can be the occasional throwback to earlier models as when, in northern Germany in December 2007, a mother killed her five sons with a combination of tranquillisers and suffocation. A social worker familiar with the case did say she appeared to have been 'gripped by religious fantasies'. But the authorities made little of this, preferring a secular explanation of mental illness and relationship breakdown. When, in the following year, Sasikala Navaneethan, a thirty-five-year-old mother of three in south London stabbed two of her children to death and attempted to do the same to the third, it was a truly modern and European child-killing – a neighbour noted that she had failed her driving test the week before. Many of us will have tasted the bitterness of a driving test failure, but few will see in it the basis for an overarching theory of parental authority over life and death. But such cases, fully as painful as the others and arguably more appalling in the absence of any grandiose justification are, strictly speaking, a distraction. These are killings, not sacrifices: there was no suggestion that Mrs Navaneethan was more likely to pass her test next time around if only she did the bidding of a ghostly voice from the Driving Standards Agency. These cases are impelled by no idea and have no very strong cultural or national identity; they cannot be fruitfully debated except in the language of forensic psychiatry. The Abrahamic principle is absent and reason will probably always be powerless to avert them, or even to understand them.

When looking for justified, ideas-based parental child-killing in Europe one has to go back a little way into the past, though not far. The last ideology to have sufficient hold over Europeans to direct not only their words and gestures but also their actions was that of mid-twentieth-century fascism and especially the messianic brand practised by the Third Reich. The Nazis are notorious as enthusiastic killers of other people, but what is less well known is that as the dream of national socialism was dying the ideology's most faithful followers became vigorous exterminators of their own children as well. It was Magda Goebbels, the model of Nazi motherhood, who showed the way by killing her six children in Hitler's Berlin bunker in the last days of the regime. She explained herself in a letter to her surviving child, Harald, an adult from an earlier marriage then safely in the care of the Allies as a prisoner of war in North Africa. The document records an essentially masochistic mind, revelling in being under the sway of an overwhelming idea and eager for operatic rituals of loyalty. Crucially, it reveals that she was incapable of accepting her personal survival beyond the death of her ideals, and equally incapable of recognising her children as separate persons in their own right. Borrowing from the language of reason, Mother Goebbels argued that life after national socialism would not be worth living '. . . and *therefore* I took the children with me'. The day after writing the letter she had a doctor sedate her children with morphine before killing all six with cyanide, an act she had earlier described to Harald as 'their salvation'. When she wrote about her loyalty to Adolf Hitler she used the plural, co-opting her children into her identifying ideology just as less fevered nationalists routinely assume that their children must share the same national identity as themselves, and as religious believers assume that their children must believe in the same gods. Another witness claimed that Magda Goebbels explicitly used the language of ownership when referring to her children: 'I belong to my husband and the children belong to me'. Their murder was the act of a proprietor as well as a matriarch.

Other members of the party did not fail to join this inspiring example. The doctor and human vivisector Ernst-Robert Grawitz, also in the bunker in the last, millennial days, slipped out just in time to return to his family home and kill everyone in it with hand grenades. Elsewhere, the mayor of Leipzig was found dead in his office with the body of his young adult daughter on the sofa opposite. One photographer's caption described her as a suicide, though without any evidence as to how she came by the poison, what she thought it was when she swallowed it, or precisely what act her parents (the third corpse in the room is assumed to be her mother) were committing when they required her to join them in death. In the open, in a Vienna park on two benches drawn together across a path, a family of four lay dead, the youngest child face down on the wooden surface, unmistakeably a bound Isaac on the pyre of his parents' obedience and possessiveness.

These regime-change killings would be repeated a few months later during the defeat of Japan, when ownership of the future was again switching dramatically from one culture and value system to another. Advancing American forces witnessed Japanese parents throwing their children off cliffs on Saipan before jumping after them, or carrying infants in their arms as they jumped together. Later, mass familicides featured prominently at the end of the Okinawa campaign, encouraged by the failing Japanese soldiery as sacrificial gestures and facilitated by the distribution of hand grenades.

There is clearly nothing culturally specific about these collective parental killings of children, mostly too young by far to understand let alone subscribe to the driving identities behind them and with nothing to fear from growing up in a post-Nazi Germany or a post-militarist Japan, neither of which turned out to be a fate worse than death. Similarly, the precise nature of the ideology and the historic period also seem irrelevant to the way human beings treat their children when their political and cultural sense of themselves is under threat. The utopian left wing has its loving killers as well as the ultra-nationalist right. The socialist community of Jonestown in Guyana ended in a spectacular suicide-murder in 1978 as soon as its charismatic leader Jim Jones had declared that 'all was lost'. One Ruletta Paul started the ball rolling by squirting poison into the mouth of her one-year-old child with a syringe. Over nine hundred died in a similar way, many of them children murdered by their parents as Jones rambled over the loudspeaker system on the subject of 'revolutionary suicide' and how any children left alive would be converted to fascism by the authorities – an outcome as unconscionable as conversion to liberalism had been to Magda Goebbels thirty-three years previously. There were only a handful of adult survivors and one of these, the seventy-nine-year-old Grover Davis, owed his rare status not to any superiority of mind, but to his deafness – he was simply unable to hear the message.

While a cluster of modern examples inevitably attracts our attention there is nothing modern about the phenomenon itself. The template for these mass parental child-killings is arguably an ancient one: the besieged Jewish fortress of Masada in the first century, the defenders of which became famous for killing themselves and their children rather than surrender to the Roman forces outside the walls, and to the Roman culture and identity they represented. The story was supposedly told to the historian Josephus by two women who survived by hiding in a cistern with five of their children. If the Masada case is in any way unusual it is in the fact that, unlike the Jim Jones cult or the events at the end of the Second World War, Masada remains an object of admiration in the context of modern Israeli nationalism. In contemporary retellings it is always the killers who are praised, not the two women who showed such a deplorable lack of commitment in saving their children.

Between the ideas of ancient Jewish zealots, defeated mid-twentieth-century fascists and a suggestible band of late 1970s utopian socialists, there is little common ground to be expected, and yet the specific details of their self-dramatising and murderous exits do undoubtedly connect them. However important their beliefs were to them, these do little to explain their actions, which we must try to understand at a deeper, if more banal level. Magda Goebbels is the more reliable guide here with her plain statement of ownership. In each case there was a choice not necessarily between death or survival, but between retaining or losing control of the child in question, either in body or mind. In addition there is the sense that the killers believed they were exercising a legitimate authority and that by exercising it lethally they could at least prevent anyone else from exercising a similar authority over their children at a later date. It is this that connects these high-profile cases through a long but unbroken continuum of psychosis to little-noticed private dramas devoid of overblown ideas or cultish leaders or directions from the heavens above. Dramas like that of Arthur Freeman who stopped his car in January 2009 on Melbourne's West Gate Bridge in the middle of morning rush hour traffic to take his daughter out of her booster seat in the back and drop her over the edge, or that of Ervin Lupoe of Wilmington, Los Angeles who had lost his job on the other side of the world only a couple of days before and killed his five children and his wife in response. Economically cornered and unable to see into a clouded future, Lupoe's situation must have felt like a personal regime-change and the question he left behind in his note was a familiar one, the question of a jealous proprietor: 'why leave our childen in someone else's hands?'

Moving eastward, we return to the historic home of the Abraham story and a region more than ordinarily hag-ridden by religions, divisive nationalisms and causes greedy for their followers' loyalty at any price. The Middle East's recent innovation in child sacrifice has been to retread the religious language of martyrdom and use it to give a false dignity to the expenditure of young lives in the conflict of the day, as well as to muddy the issue of consent by drawing in those too young to be anything other than victims. Revived as a recruiting sergeant for the Iranian side in the Iran–Iraq War, this new and superheated language of sacrifice was later exported to other groups, typically those in violent opposition to Israel. It was in 2002 that the idea made a penetrating visual impact on the rest of the world with the publication of a photograph seized by the Israeli Army from a house in Hebron, the traditional site of Abraham's tomb. It shows a Palestinian baby barely able to stand, dressed ordinarily enough except that over his shoulders and around his waist is a miniature and painstakingly hand-crafted version of military webbing. Two rows of small arms ammunition go down his chest to join a broad black belt. On the front of this belt are five stitched cloth pockets each containing a stick of mock explosive and all connected with red detonating cord. Although distributed by the Israeli authorities for their own propagandistic purposes, the authenticity of the image has not been questioned; indeed, it was obliquely confirmed by a family member, reported at the time as saying it was 'just a joke'. To the best of my knowledge the child is still alive and well, but for other children their parents' eagerness to spend them in the cause is neither a joke nor just a symbol. In June of the same year Naima al-Obeid filmed herself in Gaza propelling her twenty-three-year-old son out the door on his suicide mission. At twenty-three Mahmoud al-Obeid was certainly old enough to make decisions for himself, though with a family background like that it must be doubtful whether he ever did. Mother declared the day of her son's death to be the best day of her life, though with nine other children she still had a lot to look forward to. And that isn't much of a joke either, for a grim competitiveness developed in the Palestinian sacrifice market – one just wasn't enough. Mariam Farahat, who these days prefers to go by the name of Umm Nidal or Mother of Struggle, can boast of having used up three of her six sons in suicide attacks against Israel and may well owe her election to the Palestinian Legislative Council in 2006 to this appetite for bereavement. In this context the prodigious size of Palestinian families is not simply a matter of the low status of women or the lack of contraceptive matériel – on the most radical fringes it is a stockbreeding programme intended to deal with future military manning needs. And before any Europeans feel superior about this they should recall that France, anxiously eyeing Germany's larger population between the wars, had a very similar policy of strategic fertility. These children, in the minds of their parents, are heading for sacrifice from conception onwards.

On other continents and for other periods one could repeat these observations time and again – there is a diversity of justified child-killing, but nowhere an absence. Patriarchy and the economics of the dowry system fuel an ongoing gendercide in India, with recent demographic studies suggesting that as many as ten million deselected girls have gone missing from the Indian population over the last twenty years. In Uganda, last year's theme for Lent amongst the Christian clergy was the increase in witchcraft-related child murders. These tend not to be parental murders, but do resemble the Abrahamic model in that they are explicitly self-interested bargains – the offer of a child in return for supernaturally conferred benefits. In the Ugandan context it is typically worldly wealth rather than divine favour that is being sought. Such beliefs can travel far from their original sustaining culture and irrupt into an over-confident modernity inured to its own models of child-killing, but easily shocked by those of the third world. In 2001 police in London recovered from the Thames the headless and limbless torso of an African boy not more than six years old and traced him through the use of DNA and other evidence to an area of rural Nigeria where ritual or 'muti' killings still take place. They named him 'Adam'.

And so, as we come rattling out of the ghost train and back into the daylight, where exactly does this brisk survey of parenting malfunctions get us? Across all the boundaries of culture and age we are not only a species which harms its young, but one that loudly asserts its good reasons for doing so. The seed of Abraham has indeed descended through the generations and in many places and times has found fertile sacrifical ground in which to thrive. It is not a story confined to the past or even to a particular culture. And it is worth pointing out, if it is not already obvious, that the murderousness of the human parent is a phenomenon that also crosses the gender boundary. While feminist critiques have always been comfortable with the Abraham story because it presents a patriarchal killer, the use of his name in this chapter is nothing more than cultural arbitrariness. Had the dice of history rolled a little differently, Medea the Greek and female model would have been the name to conjure with and she would have served just as well. Seen in its totality, parental child-killing is very much an equal opportunity affair.

These acts remain rare and extreme. We look on from a distance – sympathetic, or appalled, but not personally troubled. And yet when a communal ideology is involved, a *vox Dei* of one kind or another, the frequency of parental child-killing spikes violently upwards at times of high emotion or distress and the perpetrators include those who previously looked just like us. Not sacrificing your children to deity or nation depends to a disconcerting extent on moral luck, on not finding yourself in one of those generations of whom sacrificial demands are made, be they the demands of the last days of the Third Reich, or of the disillusioned utopianism of Jonestown, or the British patriotism of 1914, or modern Palestine's self-lacerating struggle for dignity.

*

While for some parents only killing their children will do, the rest of us can agree that it is going much too far. These examples are just news stories or scenes from history. We haven't killed our children and we probably don't even know anyone who has. And when son or daughter knocks the treasured vase off the mantelpiece or spills paint on the car and finds it natural to say 'He'll really kill me now', we know that whatever that means, wherever it comes from, it doesn't mean what it says any more.

Is that it then? Have we dodged Abraham's poisonous seed? Are we, the sane and well-adjusted non-killing majority, off the hook or is all this talk of murder and sacrifice not only over-egging the argument but oversimplifying it too? After all, there are many ways of harming a child that fall short of killing and some of them, perhaps most of them, share the possessive psychopathology of the Abraham complex. In moving away from the black and white and into the more extensive grey areas it might make sense to adopt a quantitative theory of child-killing. Here the parent might choose, or be driven by a cultural impulse, not to kill off the whole child but to take a more moderate approach and kill off just some of the parts: his creativity, perhaps, her self-confidence, his capacity for trust, her sexual innocence, and most commonly of all their ability to think for themselves. Is there a more widespread, a more acceptable Abraham-lite mentality in which we might still be implicated?

The lesser, non-lethal abuses of children mandated by belief, custom or identity can also be physical and nowhere is this more obvious than in the peculiar persistence of parents' desire to mutilate their children's genitals. Only the most radical form of female circumcision has any sustainable rationale. Infibulation, the narrowing or partial closure of the vaginal opening as practised in parts of East Africa, expresses an unusual degree of contempt for the child's and the adult woman's rights, but is certainly effective in controlling her sexual behaviour. It also illustrates the deep, self-perpetuating power of social norms – for while the practice is patriarchal in the extreme it is the women who inflict it on their daughters, and their daughters on their own daughters in turn in an endless succession of acculturated self-harm. As this is a form of genital mutilation that works, one might say that it is the rational high point of the global circumcision scene – for elsewhere the practice continues on a massive scale either in the face of the obvious untruth of bogus medical claims, or as part of ethnic or religious identity rituals where the idea of there being some point to it is never lucidly formulated in the first place.

Faith-based mutilations are visited on both female and male children across wide areas of the developing and Third World, most consistently where the Abrahamic religions continue to influence the prevailing cast of mind. What is unusual is that these bloody assertions of parental authority have crossed the conceptual barrier into developed societies with high literacy rates and well-funded education systems and have found it surprisingly easy to survive there. Even those who should be able to think for themselves remain enthusiastic circumcisers, above all in the United States where male genital mutilation continues to be a weakening, but still majoritarian social norm.

A striking characteristic of first-world circumcision is its sexism. Many developed jurisdictions have sternly outlawed the genital mutilation of girls but have refused to extend the same protection to their brothers. In the United Kingdom female circumcision was made a crime in 1985, attracting a maximum of fourteen years' imprisonment. The new law specifically ruled out beliefs relating to custom and ritual as a defence, which is surprising as it is exactly this type of belief that drives the continuing lawful mutilation of boys in the United Kingdom through a network of private clinics catering to ethnic and confessional minorities, or in GP practices where the doctors share the cultural assumptions of the parents. It was in one such establishment in Reading in 2008 that Celian Monthe Noumbiwe was briskly separated from his foreskin and ushered out the door with his parents within ten minutes of the operation being completed. He was taken to hospital the next morning, but died of shock brought on by massive blood loss. He was nine weeks old. This child and others in comparable cases from the Jewish and Muslim communities should also be recognised as victims of parental sacrifice. In no sense did anyone aim at their deaths, but if their human rights had been respected they would all have lived. No crime was involved in Celian's death, nor in the one thousand other more successful circumcisions which the Reading doctors claimed to have carried out over the previous ten years. But the legality of their behaviour depends not on what they did, but on the fact that they did it only to boys — if a single patient had been female they would have risked a lengthy prison sentence. This is discrimination of a sort found nowhere else in the law codes of developed jurisdictions and it urgently calls out for reform.

If we remove the religious, ethnic and tribal impulses for marking children we are left with the enigma of the United States, the world capital of genital mutilation. In line with other developed countries the United States has criminalised female circumcision, but continues to treat the majority of its male infants very differently and acknowledges no crime when they are circumcised. In a curious sideshow it has a circumcising ally in South Korea where the wisdom of US Army doctors imparted during the Korean War carries on — circumcision as a cultural export, like baseball only more painful, less reasonable and altogether less consensual. The

American occupation of Japan from 1945 involved few doctors and so, happily, the country remained uninfected.

A historical overview of circumcision in the United States reveals a pattern in which a succession of pretended reasons for the practice comes and goes while the cutting carries on regardless. Mid-nineteenth-century anti-masturbation panics faded and were replaced by mid-twentieth-century hygiene arguments, and as these in turn have lost their plausibility a rearguard action has recently been attempted with the idea that circumcision might inhibit the transmission of the HIV virus; nothing more, in truth, than a tired recycling of the syphilophobia of the 1850s with the substitution of a more newsworthy disease. Once all pretence at reason has been abandoned there is the jealous anxiety of fathers that their sons should not be more whole than they are. The last resort is to a cringing conformism that imposes surgery so that little Brad, or Ethan or Tyler will not feel out of place in the locker room.

When the props of religion and tribalism are cut away, the pseudo-scientific alternatives prove, by comparison, to be short-lived and disposable. It matters little that the reasons for circumcision should be so easily discredited, for they were never more than cover stories for the deeply rooted compulsion of the powerful to impose themselves on the bodies of the powerless. What all these rituals or quack treatments have in common is an adult standing over a child with a knife in his or her hand, intent on spilling a little blood. The attraction perhaps should come as no surprise in a society where nearly half the adult jurors at the Californian mock trial could not condemn Abraham for holding a knife to his son's throat, let alone his foreskin.

Circumcision is a mark of ownership and domination and its social function is hard to distinguish from that of the slave-owner's brand. Those who bear the mark are daily reminded that their autonomy was compromised from the start and they will remain a part of the violator's stock long after the branding, parental generation is dead. Often, the only effective way for the victims to limit their sense of deprivation is to subscribe to a pretended normality which requires them not to protect their own children, but instead to attack them in exactly the same way.

*

When we, as parents, come to the business of leaving a permanent mark on our children, the mind will take an impression as indelibly as the body. Here, education is the tool. In modern parlance it is a word of such positive connotations that it would be hard to imagine a debate about whether or not it is a good idea. Could there be a case against education, could even the Devil's best-paid advocate come up with anything from his side of the floor? Surely not – everyone agrees that education is good, and most insist that their kind is the best of all.

For all the complexity and diversity of educational systems across the world and over time, the activity always includes two firmly opposing elements. The first now dominates the educational systems of the advanced countries and might be called emancipatory education – it concentrates on delivering verifiable information about the world and, more importantly, instilling the habit of rational and free enquiry so that the pupils can go on to discover more for themselves and to develop their own, perhaps very different ideas. In this classroom, when a pupil puts up his hand and says 'Excuse me, sir, but I think you've got that wrong and here are the reasons why', it is a sure sign that all is going well. But there is another classroom, just down the corridor in the same metaphorical school, where this sort of behaviour remains punishable. Here the aim is not to free the pupil, but to claim and possess him for subjective values and customs and to disable those parts of his intellect which might allow them later to be weakened or altogether thrown off. The teacher in this classroom is education's ever-present Mr Hyde — the hairy, claw-handed, half-man half-beast version that pops up from behind the sofa in the headmaster's study after the elixir of nation, faith or ideology has been gulped down and done its ugly work.

I think it unlikely that any actual education system exists as a pure expression of one of these strands or another; everywhere there is a mixture of the two, albeit in greatly varying proportions. Even in the village madrasa, open to the sky, where a row of boys rocks compulsively over a dusty Koran, the indoctrinator must risk imparting a dangerous degree of literacy, and thereby the chance that one day some other accessible document might come into the hands of his pupils and start to undo all his work. Across the world other children stand in the self-confident classrooms of the United States to begin their day with the regimented chant of the Pledge of Allegiance, a ritual recognised by the country's own courts as having 'the compulsory unification of opinion' as its purpose. The two systems are not equivalent, but neither are they wholly unrelated.

This other classroom, favouring the education of possession rather than of emancipation, must also be recognised as a theatre of parental sacrifice. It is by parental authority that children are sent to such places and rendered less able to understand the world as it really is, or to care as much as they ought about those who do not share their isolating world-view; a world-view they would have escaped if they had enjoyed a more liberating education. As for this amounting to another parental sacrifice, the idea will seem more plausible if we reflect that the explanation for the young suicide bomber, or patriotic soldier or committed terrorist is not to be found in their violent ends but only in tracking backwards to the classrooms of Hamas in the Palestinian territories, or of Prussian nationalists in the Weimar Republic, or of the jealously segregated school system in Northern Ireland. The purpose of sending a child to a school like this is to lay on his mind deep marks of opinion and sentiment, marks that may be softened in later life but are rarely erased. The purpose, one might say, is the circumcision of the mind.

*

Are these connections real, or is the notion of a link between the extremes of parental violence and the more everyday violations of our children's rights merely fanciful? Is it no more than rhetorical play to find two expressions of the same darkness in the cutting off of a foreskin and the cutting of a throat, or to juggle comparisons between the scarring of the body and the scarring of the mind? I don't aim to be a bullying advocate and will happily leave you to decide for yourselves

on the issue of common culpability, let alone on the relative
weight of your own guilt or innocence towards your own
children. But what I will say is that how you see the world
depends very much on the life you have lived, and when a
man comes home one day to find that home empty and his
children gone and their futures damaged and their chances
in life cut down by one of their own parents, then some
truths become clear which previously were hidden.

I have looked around the world, briefly, casually, at some
of the ways in which one generation most gravely mistreats
the next. It is not a reassuring picture. After such a review a
good night's sleep is hardly to be expected and I can't help but
wonder if that hypothetical monster I started with is still
under the bed after all – or if not under the bed, then hidden
deep in the animal bodies of Father Dear and Mother Dear,
in the ancient parts that still pray to old Abraham and whatever it is he stands for. As a principle, I fear he is still alive and
well – the busy patron saint of all those who would destroy
what is real and precious in obedience to the illusory and the
worthless.

*

It is early March 2009. It is now. It is almost six years since I
have seen my children.

I stretch and push my chair back from the desk. I come up
for air. I click on PRINT and then pace the flat as the familiar
rhythm plays in the background and the sheets slide out one
by one. I stand by the window and gaze out across the town
to the dead volcano and to the hill with its bankrupt temple,

its blind observatory tower and on its western shoulder, cut out against a bleak, snow-white sky, a choragic rotonda thrown up by some old friends in memory of a second-rate philosopher no one has read for a hundred and fifty years. The illusory, the worthless. The higher ground is grey with snow and isolated flakes are still sinking through the air. On the windowsill I see the crippled telephone and beside it the scrap of paper with the long number that would, until a few months ago, connect me to my children's voices. It is dead now, and leads only to a recorded message which tells me, in Japanese, that I am wasting my time. But I still call it anyway. The printer falls silent.

It's late in the evening before I read this chapter, wondering which parts I really believe, which parts are for show, which parts are my own cherished delusions. I start to check a few of the facts and while doing this I go looking once again for the image of the Palestinian baby suicide bomber. There are many versions, and as I scroll through them, alert for fresh exhibits in the depravity museum, something half familiar, half new catches my eye. I lean forward to get a better look and then click on the image to enlarge it. It is a boy, perhaps not yet three years old. He is dressed in a fantasy short-trousered version of a khaki uniform with plastic medals pinned on his chest and plastic dog tags around his neck to help identify his corpse on the battlefield. Though a little impressionistic in some details it is, unmistakeably, intended to be the uniform of the United States Army. It has obviously not been home made like its Palestinian equivalent, but manufactured and offered for sale in a shop. Perhaps many thousands have been made and sold. The boy has a slightly confused and anxious expression as he looks past the camera seeking reassurance from, presumably, the loving parent behind it; the one who bought the gift, the one who dressed this infant as a soldier.

3 *How did it really start?*

Is there a day in your life utterly different from all the others, not just one of several that stand out, but one that is quite alone and unique, one that you would save from a burning house of memories without a moment's debate or hesitation, one that – so far as anyone can predict – will be with you at the end as bright and clear as if it were yesterday?

I have never asked anyone this question face to face; with all its implications and its intimacy it is hard to imagine a situation where it would not be intrusive. Hard also to imagine that some of the answers would not be lies, some fictions, some others evasions followed by silence and a distant expression, impossible to read. Perhaps there are even people for whom there would not be any obvious answer, just a furrowing of the brow as they struggle to pick out some thing convincing from the flat expanse of a life that never really started. For the parent it is easier. Whatever the parent says out loud I believe their answer is always the same: that unique day is the birth day of their first child. That is my answer, though I offer it with apologies to my second son and the hope that he will understand that even the best of things can't happen all at once.

And which day, in particular, was it for me? The 1st of May 1997 – a day of some standing in British history, election day, the end of a right-wing government that had come to power when I was a schoolboy of fourteen and which had produced in me a sense of alienation for every moment of its rule, a day which created a club whose members will recognise each other decades hence by their common understanding of the phrase 'up for Portillo', a day that is already yellowing in the memory and has its own historical quality, more remote and distinctive than might be expected after the passage of a mere fourteen years. All that for me and more besides — fatherhood day, the day when things really did change for the better.

We did not own a car — living, in material terms at least, not by the norms of the late 1990s but as a couple of some forty years previously might have lived, saving for what others called the basics, calculating with small sums of money and an eye on the end of the month. Home, purchased with Tomoko's always mysterious financial resources, was a two-up, two-down redbrick terraced house built ninety or a hundred years before to house the workers of Reading's more paternalistic employers. For us it was conveniently located, a quarter of a mile from the maternity department of the Royal Berkshire Hospital to whose antenatal classes we dutifully walked in the last two months of the pregnancy. There, through a series of late winter and early spring evenings we sat in a semicircle of straight-backed chairs covered in a two-colour range of wipe-clean plastics and were told things that in any healthier society no one would need to be told.

'Breastfeeding! Douglas — how do you know when baby has had enough?'

The room is stuffy and overheated, the windows black. I am fagged out from having spent all day selling wine to middle-class alcoholics from the galley benches of a lightless call centre. Just at this moment I am struggling to care – but I shrug and take a stab at this pointless question.

'He just stops. Maybe stops and falls asleep?'

'Yes!'

Our midwife instructor has the brightness of a primary school teacher and I get the impression this is such a brilliantly meritorious answer that she is about to bear down on me with a gold star. Even then I must have asked myself how we got to this state, how we ended up in a society where such an absurd exchange is even possible.

It was during that penultimate class on the last day of April 1997, on election eve, that we were all startled to have our obstetric education interrupted by a commercial pitch from a baby milk salesman. The midwife reminded us in strained tones that breast was best and that nothing we were about to hear about powdered formula amounted to medical advice but, well – would we mind sitting through it anyway? The guy did his thing: chirpy, upbeat, commerce's variety act. At one level cynicism always sounds the same – when someone is addressing you solely with their own interests in mind their words, whatever they might be, carry with them a silent, smiling bat's squeak of 'fuck you' that protects those who can pick it up and identify it for what it is. I heard it loud and clear that evening and assume money must have changed hands at some remote and rarely scrutinised point along the line. I won't say the salesman swung it for Labour in Reading West the next day – but I'm sure he didn't do any harm.

We wander home at a leisurely eight-and-a-half-months-pregnant pace. Reading, in truth, is a charmless town and few people can ever be sorry to leave it. But for me there is a trick of memory when I look back on that evening walk. The road is tree-lined. I have pasted in larger, grander trees from another nearby location; I know it's inaccurate, but it's how I see it now, memory always being more of an artist than a historian. Over the winter the trees have been brutally pollarded but now they are fighting back with vigorous new green, almost touching across the roadway at the top. We must have made a slightly comic pair – myself over-tall and narrow, something like an old Daumier caricature, and Tomoko a short fertile sphere stretched just about as tight as nature will allow. Holding hands? Maybe, but it's hard to summon that image now – memories get erased as well as changed. And so there we were, the three of us, a retouched Hansel and Gretel heading through the trees on a warm spring night.

We never got to the last antenatal class and remain ignorant of its contents to this day. I don't suppose it would have made any difference. Reality overtook theory some time about midnight. A rustling, a disturbance, an elbow in the ribs.

'Get up.'

Me sleepy, reluctant, sceptical, male –

'Mmm? What? Are you sure?'

'Don't ask me if I'm sure – get up!'

A taxi is called. The driver is a fatherly character in late middle years, long used to the night shift on this particular beat. I catch his eye in the rear-view mirror and he is keen to play his part in the nativity drama.

'Ah,' he says to us, 'going in for the firstborn?'

I say yes and he tells us that he remembers it all very well himself. He keeps up a reassuring stream of conversation as he drives with exaggerated care over the speed bumps. His own children must be adults now and he talks back to us plainly and intensely, as someone reporting from the far side of a great adventure – one which, I sensed, he had come through safely and well.

'Life is never the same again, that's for sure. Everything will change now – *everything*.'

We pull up under the canopy of the reception area and as I pay the small fare he looks straight at me and says, as if knowingly to someone who is about to embark on a new and less certain generation of fatherhood.

'Good luck.'

I remember the view from the maternity suite, how the windows looked out on the new growth of the trees and then, above this green foundation, held only the orange black of the urban night sky, a colour I hardly noticed changing and lightening as 1 May 1997 dawned. It must have been the third or even a higher floor, and so there must have been a lift and an exit into a linoleum corridor and an arrow pointing under the buzzing fluorescent lights towards the locked security door, a first hint of the world of danger the parent enters, an implication of thefts, kidnaps and long-forgotten newspaper sensations.

I press the intercom buzzer while Tomoko leans against the wall as another contraction arrives. There is a lengthy silence. I look up at the lens of a security camera and wonder if there is anyone watching our fuzzy black and white image. I press the buzzer again and someone appears – a matronly

midwife of the old school who lets me know at once that I am
of the invisible gender as she elbows me aside and takes
charge. It is this same woman who performs the first examin-
ation a short while later. Tomoko and I have been resting in
the triage suite, the only couple there on a quiet night. We
listen to the amplified heartbeat of our unborn child, a loud
rhythmic whisper pulsing through the speaker of the foetal
monitor. And there she is again, standing beside the bed,
pulling on a latex glove and smearing two fingers with lubri-
cating jelly. When the first severe glare in my direction fails
to shift me from my wife's side she asks very sharply if I would
like to step outside. I ignore her and ask Tomoko what she
wants, but we both feel overborne by this bossy, uniformed
figure and I am pushed away. The distance, only a few feet
and a thin partition wall, felt oddly important, even
distressing. But what has remained most clearly in the
memory is the shock of the midwife's assumed authority to
penetrate my wife while at the same time being so anxious to
remove from the scene the person who – in part at least –
started this pregnancy. What were her motives, what were
her thoughts or concerns as she went about her work in what
was, presumably, her usual way? I can't say, but this minor
irritant has connected in my mind with later events and
taken on a greater significance, a fragment of evidence about
a society in which it is normal to distance men from their
children, sometimes even before they are born.

What unfolded over the next eight hours proved to be of
no great medical interest and resulted in only a few more
ticked boxes in the yellow folder of notes Tomoko had been
carrying with her for the last several months. The midwives

and the doctor will not recall this routine procedure, and there is nothing useful I can say about an experience that exists almost wholly beyond words – one either knows from one's own life, or does not know at all. Five or six hours in, an epidural was called for. This took about an hour to organise and when some extra kit and staff finally appeared a nurse fished around and said 'I don't think there's much point, really.' And so it proved. A little while later I was the second person in the world – an instant after the midwife – to see the top of this child's head, well supplied with dark brown hair. And then the quick slithering end and that common-place but also central image of any human life – the bloodied new infant held up, and the astonishment and the brief, seizing fear before the first gasp and the sharp new voice is heard.

It is a boy – news to his parents, who have taken care not to know in advance. It is Satomi, as I have come to call him, the little runner who would beat someone six years later at the school sports day just before my part in his life would come to an end.

'He looks a little shocked,' says the midwife.

Not unreasonable, I thought, given what he had just been through.

'I'll give him a bit of oxygen.'

She prepares to take him across the room to an incubator and as the umbilical cord is severed I find that another, less visible, has become attached to me and I am drawn after them as forcefully as if it were real, barely able to stop myself from asking where this woman is going, what on earth she thinks she is doing with my son. In a minute I have him, oxygenated and neatly wrapped. It would be easy to say, especially as a writer with the profession's defining weakness of preferring a good phrase to the truth, that this cord has not been weakened by years of absence or thousands of miles of separation – and so I check conscientiously with my sentiments before finishing this sentence and find that it is, after all, true.

In the standard dramatisations of birth the newborn is held by the mother: it is what we expect. On this occasion it was different, as it must be on many others too, if only to allow for the practicalities of tending to a woman who is more in need than the dazed father. I was the one sitting on a chair by the side of the bed, holding our son for the first half-hour of his life, asking the midwife about the milk spots on the tip of his nose, turning the tiny plastic bracelet around his wrist to read the world's first label, 'Galbraith – Boy', and noticing that it was made so that it could only be cut off with scissors or a knife, a precaution against mishaps, changelings, and child-stealers. It is, of course, a key memory for me now, standing out in sharp clarity while so much else has become vague or has vanished altogether. I see it, alternately, from two different points of view. The first is the factual one, the view from where I actually was, looking down at Satomi in my arms, seeing how still and quiet he was and being misled into thinking how easy it would all be. The other is the composed view, that slightly out-of-body perspective with which we often regard our past selves, standing on an old box of the mind to get a bit of height. There I am, the new parent absorbed in his new child, a slightly dark pair of figures as they are seen against a wide ribbon of brilliant turquoise that runs horizontally across the image, the May Day morning light coming through the hospital windows. Highlights fire off the edges of medical equipment and the standing figure of the midwife as she completes her notes. From the left, halfway up, Tomoko's stirruped ankle and foot just cross the frame as she submits to the attentions of the obstetrician whose bending, blue-clad back fills the lower left quadrant. If I were a painter, this is what my mind would give you rather than these words. In the context of western art it would be a rare image; some might even say there was something wrong with it. For a start the gender of the person holding the child would seem odd, even provocative. More generally the observer might feel that the whole angle of view was wrong and that the solution would be to shift it back to the left, to centre it on the mother and thus return to the conventions of the Madonna and Child leaving, at most, a male elbow or shoulder to intrude from the right. It is hard to convey what my imagined picture is like precisely because there are so few other examples with which to compare it.

Gaps appear in my memory, uncertainties – like those zigzag lines that flicker across the screens of cartoon televisions before a character hits them to bring the world back into shape. The next picture is of the town itself, sunny, warm, busy, vigorously recovered from the recession of the early 1990s. It cannot really have been remade since the day before, but it appears inside my head in fresh colours and scents, everything invested with the subjective magic of a new importance. I constantly feel the urge to stop and tell some passer-by of this momentous addition to the human population, or perhaps clamber on to a piece of street furniture and make a general announcement from amid the crowded election posters. I am smiling to myself as I go about the errands Tomoko has set me. I attract attention – evidently transformed from the outside as well.

I must have spent the afternoon back at the hospital, and then home on my own to pick up a polling card and walk a few streets to the other novelty of the day: voting for a British government, for a changed future in which I now had an expanded and less selfish stake. This I did not want to miss, not a moment of it, and so a small television was sitting in the corner of the room, bought for the purpose – my generation's 'coronation set', a Japanese orange box serving as its make-shift cross-cultural plinth. The result was not in doubt, but it still needed to be seen to be believed, to finally banish the fear that the electorate would once again timidly duck the obvious choice as they had five years before.

For me, and others of my age, the night bookended one of our earliest political memories – a blue-suited Margaret Thatcher taking power in 1979 and quoting some moralising flannel from St Francis of Assisi with a bug-eyed self-certainty that turned out to be a more reliable predictor of her behaviour in office. For anyone thirty-one years old in May 1997, all their adult years had been Conservative years. Emerging as I did, by a sociologically obscure process, from an unthinkingly Conservative family, there had never been any private asylum from the public unease. Something intangible had built up in my system, a steadily rising concentration of pollutants which had oozed from the Falklands War, the miners' strike, the toleration of mass unemployment, the denial of the existence of society itself, and the promotion into the upper reaches of public life of a parade of self-servers, bribe-takers and a brace of future convicted criminals. With a slightly exaggerated sense of occasion, I sat down to watch what promised to be more of a revolution than an ordinary election. I sat down also in the expectation of seeing something that would make me feel a little cleaner.

It was more than anyone had expected, or dared hope for. I should have been exhausted, but was kept wide awake through the night by a series of vengeful shots of adrenalin as seat after Conservative seat was lost – an astonishing 178 in all, not a single gain, elimination in Scotland and Wales and a collapse of the right wing's constituency not seen since the second quarter of the nineteenth century. From the next house in the terrace an increasingly delirious victory party grew ever louder as the results rolled in. At the twin moral high points of the drama – the defeat by an independent candidate of the corrupt backbencher Neil Hamilton, and then of the former Defence Secretary Michael Portillo – the noise from this gathering first hushed to an eager silence and then exploded in cheers, bellowing, stamping of feet and the ricocheting of champagne corks off the shared wall. The scale of the victory was such that the Labour Party had won at least two terms of government at a single stroke. It felt like a good time for my son to be born – a slightly precious thought perhaps, and a naive one in retrospect.

Early on Friday morning I watched the new Prime Minister arrive at Downing Street to be greeted by the public and by his senior colleagues, memorably rigid with embarrassment as a PR officer bullied them into moving to the beat of the campaign song 'Things Can Only Get Better'. They clearly didn't like the idea, but went along with it anyway – a warning for the future. No schlock from a medieval saint this time, just the ordinary clichés of change and renewal – eager talk about a new day, the usual stuff about dawn inspired, no doubt, by the fact that it was indeed dawn on 2 May 1997. There were no complaints as the words fell on fertile, relieved and vulnerable ground. I can't recall the detail of my thoughts at the time, but I was surely too old a virgin voter to take it all at face value. Some of the optimism did turn out to be justified, but as the radio plays in the background and I hear Blair's voice as he gives his version to the Chilcot inquiry into the Iraq War in 2010, it's hard now to reconstruct that mood of thirteen years ago; hard also to imagine that the British people, for a generation, will ever be as unguardedly hopeful again.

What then? A failed attempt at a couple of hours' rest, a pacing, impatient breakfast and then the leafy walk to the hospital to collect Tomoko and our new son and return to what was, for the first time in our tenancy, a family home. It was Friday and I hadn't slept since Wednesday. I was in that state prized by interrogators after they have shone lights in captives' eyes and played loud music in their ears for days on end. I was unsure of what was real, and had the illusion that the ground beneath my feet had become soft and was pushing back against my steps, helping my progress which became fluid and strangely accelerated, as if the pavement was a moving walkway in an invisible airport. I remember waiting to cross the road, puzzling over the lights and the cars and sluggishly struggling back to reason with the thought that I must not be run over because now it really would matter. And that was my wide-awake, seventy-two-hour day of days – pin-sharp and colourfast for as long as I remember anything.

Two years later and we were there again: the same linoleum in the same corridor, the same buzzing lights. Only this time I had the busy, curious Satomi for company, running up and down, climbing all over the seats at one in the morning, unmoved as I tell him that the sound coming through the thin partition wall is the amplified heartbeat of his unborn brother.

By this stage the family was already very troubled; in truth, it had been since before Satomi was born. This second night birth meant that Satomi and I went home together for some sleep and breakfast together the next morning in an atmosphere of calm and harmony that he had hardly ever experienced. I was absent from my second son's birth because I was looking after my first. Although I regret that, this arrival is marked out just as vividly in my mind because of the revelation it brought of how family life could have been were it not constantly degraded by the failure of the adult relationship. Then, as on a handful of other occasions, I remember Tomoko's absence as an abrupt and dramatic change in the weather – an outbreak of sunshine on me and my children, all the more brilliant for its rarity. Quite possibly Tomoko has similar happy memories of my own absences. The thought allows more than a little sympathy for those who bolt for single-parent life, licensed by a society that has raised them to talk of their own satisfaction as a matter of right. Breakfast with Satomi, father and two-year-old son, playing at the modern

one-parent household for a few hours, sensing the difference in everything as if a droning and constant sound had
just been cut off, or an ever-present taint cleared from the
air. Perhaps from now on, for many of us, singleness will be
as good as it gets.

The telephone rings. It's Tomoko and she sounds good.
Everything has gone smoothly and she's proud of the citation
in her notes where it reads Pain Relief: None.

'And the baby?'

'Everything's all right. Come and see us.'

I get Satomi organised and strap him into the car. The
days of buses and taxis were over as the family had ascended
to a clapped-out Peugeot, new to us with a six-figure
mileage and the defensive habit of belching blue smoke
with the density of a dreadnought evading its pursuers at
sea. In a few minutes we were at the maternity ward, and
then in the room itself. Another nativity scene as I peer into
the transparent plastic crib and hold up an indifferent
Satomi to view his sibling. I'm not sure what I'm looking at
and so I ask —

'Boy or girl?'

I am told to look and so I do, reaching again for the tiny
pink wrist and the security tag, turning it until I see, without
surprise, the words 'Hanazaki — Boy'.

And so there is the first sight of the full cast: two adults
and two little bones of contention, a fragile quartet of
humanity destined for separation — certainly, there could
never have been any other outcome. And yet, what does
any of this explain? Nothing, I would say, or not much — and
if there is an explanation, all that this bare narration of

events suggests is that it does not lie here but further in the past.

*

There is a convention that the adolescent journal — the journal no one persists with for more than a year or two — should start with a grand sense of location. After a name, a street and a town and then a country too, there follows the rest of the address, along the lines of 'the earth, the solar system, the Milky Way, the Universe', the whole flourish ending with a rank of passionate exclamation marks. No one could question its accuracy, nor its keen appetite for completeness. There's a laudable determination to follow things to their source and a sense that explanations can never really be local, that the big answers, the ones worth having, are all to be found far away, or in the past at some distant point when someone, or something loaded the dice. I find myself back in that mindset, needing to make sense of things, aggressively suspicious of everyone else's version and convinced that the proper direction for such an enquiry is backwards.

The issue of names comes first to mind, and the small history of their changes away from the innocent 'boy' of the hospital bracelet, followed by the telling drift from one parental surname to the other. When Satomi examined his little brother for the first time in late April 1999, he was still only half Satomi and half Finlay, his original, agreed first name — Finlay Satomi Hanazaki Galbraith in full, much to the annoyance of the registrar, who tore up her first effort at a birth certificate and treated me to a very disapproving look. For the first months the agreement held, though it is doubtful whether his mother ever silently referred to him with this most un-Japanese sound. Then the slippage began, a series of minor border incidents and carefully manipulated misunderstandings that history tells us are the usual preamble to full-scale invasion. Japanese steadily expanded its territory as the domestic language, and if one is speaking Japanese anyway did it not make sense to use a Japanese name, whatever had been agreed? You can agree whatever you like with the obsessed. The problem is, it never stays agreed for long.

I worked out later that the kindergarten staff had accepted instructions to change my son's name without consulting me. They were, naturally enough, all women and stand out now in my mind as the earliest members of a growing female Freemasonry who always knew where their loyalties lay when it came to the business of unbending a father's grasp, finger by finger, from any disputed child. It would be paranoia to see any planning in this – I'm sure there was none; no crime, no conspiracy, no drama. Only the settled and unreflective unfairness of one gender to another, the normality of altering a child's name on the unquestioned say-so of the female parent alone. It was my first encounter with a sort of structural injustice that feminist critiques have been so adept at recognising and deploring elsewhere, though in this instance it wasn't patriarchy, but its mirror image.

The pattern was repeated more intimately and more disturbingly in my own family, very much a majority female unit and one which my father had long since decided was best dealt with by spending more time at the office, a strategy that has become easier to understand, or at least to accept with every passing year. A visit, then – a journey north to Scotland, to the frigid and barely habitable wastes of Tomoko's imagination, to the strange customs, the questionable hygiene, the potentially untrustworthy wildlife, the unswallowable diet consisting exclusively of the parts that all other cultures throw away, the ceaseless demented bagpiping and, worst of all, the in-laws. Who would not be anxious, who could not sympathise? But it is one of these tense occasions in particular that I remember, or that part of it anyway that relates to names. What stood out was the odd consistency with which my first son – then wandering in the nominative no man's land of Finlay/Satomi, Satomi/Finlay – was referred to exclusively by his Japanese name, its European predecessor scrupulously avoided. As this involved several people at once it had the appearance of organisation, of being the result of a decision taken by a group who, though they outnumbered Tomoko culturally, did not do so in terms of gender.

Later, much later when it didn't matter any more and I was searching the house for a trace of where my children might be in Japan, I found not the address I was hoping for but the answer to this puzzle. Tomoko was always a meticulous correspondent, adjusting her imperative, slightly antique style until she achieved just the effect she wanted – that sweet spot between an editorial from *The Times of India* and the bellowings of a North Korean newsreader. For a ukase on the issue of names every detail had to be right and there would be several drafts – here was one of them, a cluttered sheet of A4 heavily worked with scratchings-out and over-writing as she thought up new rhetorical escalations. It took time to work out what it was, but in the end it was clear: a letter to Satomi's grandmother, to the distaff side of the in-laws, a toxic little billet-doux, mother to mother, on the subject of names, an invitation to a conspiracy against the male and one which, apparently, was accepted.

These days, the local half of my children's extended family doesn't know quite what to call the absent ones and oscillates between East and West as if in awkward, but never openly admitted apology for an act of collaboration. I have added to the problem by wandering offside. For me also, Finlay is now Satomi, aloud, in company, and more candidly in my dreams as well – not out of surrender, but from a continuing faith in the belief that names aren't really what matters, that they never justify the wars fought over them. I suppose there must be something wrong with me here – whatever organ it is that causes people to care whether a patch of territory is called the Malvinas or the Falklands, Israel or Palestine or that leads Scotsmen abroad to tire their new acquaintances with unwanted explanations of why they're not English doesn't seem to work in me. I suspect it just isn't there at all and even now I can't bring myself to regret that. From an evolutionary point of view I should be a rare specimen, humanity's doomed red squirrel being gradually eased out of existence by more territorially aggressive grey cousins. Perhaps what lurks in me are some of those old-style Neanderthal genes, the more laid-back version of humanity that could never quite get organised for a fight, the last member of which had his skull bashed in with a rock by a *Homo sapiens* after a dispute about what to call the rock. But

I'm not so sure — evolution is a long game, and our mongrel children are everywhere.

And so, two years after his arrival, Satomi — as we may now consistently call him for the rest of this book — acquired his little brother, the round-faced, loving and even tempered Makoto; Mako-chan to those who know him well. He too had a western name, but now buried more discreetly in the middle of his lengthy multicultural label where it would not be much seen, or heard — another compromise that turned out not really to be a compromise at all.

And my own role in this, my responsibility? Eavesdrop on this: lunch in a restaurant in Glasgow, a break in the publicity work for a novel through which I am being expertly shepherded by the woman sitting opposite. The year is 2000, my boys three and one year old, are hundreds of miles away to the south living in the house that fiction built. Only one thing remains, one very brief exchange. Somehow the subject of names has come up, their mutability

'And don't you mind?' she asks.

It's a tough question. I push whatever it was I ordered around the plate.

'Well,' I say, 'I do. It just seems there isn't much I can do about it.'

How does that sound now? Just how useful would that be for the prosecution? We've all got one — our own little Nixon tape.

*

Further back then, wider as the questions ripple out — back to when there were not yet any names, no staked claims. It's dark again, there are pictures on a screen. Not the microfilm reading room this time, not the cinema you pay for and never really care about – this is different, one of the very few modern, technological experiences that is neither an entertainment nor one more minor increment to our convenience. This matters. There are three figures, softly lit in greenish grey, expectant silhouettes against this single source of light, a suggestion of the miraculous in some High Renaissance painting. Tomoko is the rounded hill in the foreground. Her belly is slick with gel and the expert, the one who knows, this uniformed sorcerer moves over it a device like the receiver of a telephone. She doesn't look at what she's doing but rather at the screen, taking cues as to where to move her detector. Snowy grey forms emerge and vanish. Tomoko and I stare at them intently, fearfully – two primitives straining to read our fate in the movement of flames, or the leaves on a tree. The sonographer freezes the image and takes a measurement. She makes a note and a neutral, monosyllabic noise. You can't tell with these people – they convey disaster and reassurance with the same tone. However a sentence starts, you never know how it's going to end and so you're always on edge, as one might be in the company of a dog known to bite without warning.

The image shifts again.

'There – you see?'

And we do see – the fast, steady flicker of a heart. The movement shoots adrenalin into our own adult hearts that jump in response.

'It's all right?'

'Fine,' says the technician, the professional, 'absolutely fine.'

I breathe out and my pulse slows, Tomoko's too, no doubt.

The image clouds and then wanders, displaying things that she understands but we do not.

'Let's see if we can get a nice one for you to take home.'

She moves the probe a little and then angles it so that all at once everything on the screen makes sense. A baby appears, so clear and sudden that it takes me by surprise and I gasp. There it is – the head, the arms folded with the hands up close to the chin, the body with its see-through ribcage and its beating heart, the legs and feet neatly tucked in. It is the first sight of our first child, the modern world's Annunciation.

She makes a last few notes as the image prints out on a small three by three inch sheet. I compose myself just in time for the house lights coming up. She closes her folder and places it out of reach, firmly on her side of the proceedings. It's for them, not us.

'And do you want to know the sex?'

'No!'

I jump in too hard and fast, keen to forestall any accidental disclosures. I can't deny that I have been examining the screen for a clue – it's what existentialists call bad faith, the hope that a random interruption will excuse you from having to follow your own rules. It's what the rest of us call having it both ways.

'Oh,' she says when I admit this, 'you won't know unless I tell you.'

So the rules still apply. Tomoko and I discussed this question in advance and arrived at a solemn policy – a strange one for me, never before having consciously chosen ignorance over knowledge. There was a time when I could not have imagined such a thing — saying no to knowledge was a revolution in my values, another belated step into the complexity and submission of adulthood.

I knew that in other parts of the world even to ask the question is forbidden, and to answer it is a crime. In India and in China too the foresight that ultrasound scanning brings is a death sentence for the female foetus. Police raid the clinics and impound the machines, staff are arrested, the pregnant 'mystery shopper' testifies. Typically, it all comes to nothing. Friends in high places make a few telephone calls, appreciation is shown and the girls keep on vanishing. The law is a well-meaning but unenforceable gesture, especially when it so often relates to the unspoken — the prohibited words are never uttered; an expression will suffice, a lethal tone of regret in the voice. As for those who breach the womb's confidentiality, they can always tell themselves that they are merely sparing everyone the unpleasantness of a post-partum solution. In the streets young men on mopeds carry mobile units and make appointments at addresses in the less prosperous quarters. Just recently the brochures of western medical imaging companies have begun to offer the hand-held scanner, and there's sure to be a strong export market in certain regions. Some of this I knew at the time; enough, at least, to feel the political and cultural charge of the question. Even so, my very definite 'no' was not a political action, but a personal one. What could the motive be for saying 'Yes. Tell me, I want to know'? Surely, it could only be because one cares about the answer, because one has an emotional investment in that answer being one word or another. There will be medical circumstances where this makes perfect sense, but with those exceptions I believe this must be a mistake. However skilfully one lies about it, the memory of how one's heart leapt or sank on the first hearing of this news will remain and attach itself in later years, if only by the faintest traces, to whoever turned out to be not-the-daughter, or not-the-son you would have preferred – not the one who would have been less ambiguously welcomed into the world. Gender is a sort of name too, a caste in some parts and these days increasingly a political allegiance, a nation of the sexual world one can be for or against. If it had a flag, friends and enemies would divide beneath it. All that enquiring about an unborn child's gender does is start the process of discrimination a little sooner, to erode the unconditionality of love. I don't have a

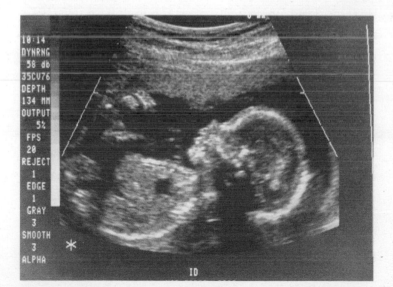

daughter, but it mattered very much to me that I should leave the ultrasound suite believing that I might have one soon, and not caring either way.

When was that day, that sudden, staggering image of life on a screen? I have to pause and count back from Satomi's birthday to work it out. It must have been towards the end of 1996. The leafless trees would have made the town more miserable than usual and I see it as icy and the light as failing already in the mid-afternoon. Fourteen years ago — I want to get hold of it, but there is already so little left. I abandon the keyboard and catch a bus into town to a library where I peer back at November 1996 as it slithers by on another microfilm reader. It's a world of vanished currencies where the goods of life are still traded in Deutschmarks and francs. Vanished potentates too, the men we used to talk about — Yeltsin, Kohl, Chirac and Mrs Clinton's husband. For the most part it's all just yesterday, suggesting that our son was about to be born into one of the better periods — a becalmed, historyless blank in which nothing much changed and all the most intense memories would be private. There had been another record session on Wall Street while in Britain the Labour Party — in its last months of opposition — was taking aim at the 'fat cats' pay bonanza. The fearfulness of the modern parent was anatomised through the story of a girl who died after taking an Ecstasy tablet. Beside it, in a long single column down the right-hand side, is the tale of a mother of triplets who adored the two boys and tortured, broke and nearly murdered the girl before someone rescued her just in time — Gabrielle. Did I read it, think about it? Was it a part of my 1996?

And me? A call-centre worker in boomtown, driving the

oldest car in the jam. At home sat a recent letter in a drawer — the worldliness of a literary agent, terms, percentages, all the grown-up language that took a still largely unwritten novel more seriously than I did myself. Would this be a way out, or up? No, I would have said if you had asked me then. Not a chance.

We stand together in the gloom outside the hospital, a sheet of newsprint blowing by. We have stopped on the pavement because we cannot go any further without looking again at the ultrasound picture to check that it has not vanished or changed. Tomoko puts it away quickly to protect it from the rain that starts to fall. Was it better then, was that the point at which it might still have worked — before things were named? I'm doubtful. It is not the names, but submission to the inner voice of race and nation, the insistent demand for one label rather than another. That, surely, must already have been there, too small, or hazy, or sly to show up on the screen, but a defect all the same, a bad gene of the parental mind. If the sonographer was a poor clairvoyant it's because she was looking in the wrong place. To tell this family's future she should have turned her machine on the parents.

*

Back again, down another layer — only a few months this time, into the warmth and the green of summer. The house has not yet been bought — nothing to put in it — and the scene is the bedroom in a rented apartment in the grounds of Reading University. I would have been called a couple of days before, summoned from Cambridge where I still lived in a Bateman Street rooming house; or Batman Street as the adjusted sign at the end of the road always had it. The place was not quite a slum, and not quite anything else – a low-cost repository for the damaged and the resigned and the occasional interloper economising while on the way up. I was one of the more long-term residents and subsisted in the back room, recommended by nothing save for a sizeable marble mantelpiece, proof that it had not always been mean, and the laburnum close by the window which for two weeks every year would fill the air with yellow light and gild the page of whatever I was reading. The establishment received few visitors and its doormat bore little in the way of communications from the outside world beyond the housing benefit cheque and the rejected manuscript. There was a payphone in the hall and a coin-operated meter for electricity. It's me on the phone.

'Well of course I want to, but I might get some work on Saturday. What about next weekend?'

I have not been paying attention. I have missed the real and unspoken message.

'No,' says Tomoko very firmly. 'It must be this weekend. It *must* be – you understand?'

It is an invitation of the utmost significance.

And so there we are, lying together on the narrow bed, a late summer morning and the room too hot under the shallow, slated bungalow roof even for a single sheet. My memory's camera eye looks down from an upper corner, the dusty vertex in which sagging fairground balloons come to rest before losing their helium. Tomoko is a little short to be one of Modigliani's models, but the shape is right, and the colour not far off. The contrast of those dark patches against the not so pale skin is very clear and perfectly composed. Beside her, I am an unlovely figure and it might appear, to a snapshot observer at least, that I have found more than I deserve. We are exhausted, damp, rich. This is the life we call art, living for the bright and thoughtless instant as the animals we are, mating in summer for spring young, briefly clean and simple in the midst of modern lives that are, otherwise, lives of almost total artificiality. The window is open and only the net curtain screens it. Outside, a dense, black-green cotoneaster has attracted so many bees that we can hear their steady hum from where we lie. Tomoko stretches.

'Well,' she says, 'at least we'll be able to tell him he was beautifully conceived.'

At least? Why at least? But that's not what matters now, not what must be recorded – it's the rest that is important. It would be hard to prove, or even to make much of a case for it, so all I can do is retreat briefly from reason and call it a conviction about what is important and what is not. There are likely to be times in many lives when coming across such a piece of personal prehistory, in an old book perhaps, could have the power to make all the difference. We should know if we have been beautifully conceived.

But this is already late in the story, long after iceberg and *Titanic* have converged. Back again, then, a longer step this time, into a summer of the late 1980s. The scene is set for a costume drama of the late sixteenth century, though the players are all in modern dress – perhaps it's just a rehearsal. It's an Oxbridge college, one of those photogenic ones you see on TV as a backdrop to lives either idyllic or deranged, but never much in between. This is not the undergraduate world, but that of the research students, a minor United Nations of more or less formidable intellects, some ambitious and busy, others mired in anomie, the asylum seekers hoping to fend off reality for another year or two before the brute finally kicks the door in and makes something happen. In Act I time passes and nothing happens. In Act II more time passes. The whole affair has the appearance of being cooked up by an East European experimental dramatist of the late 1950s. The joke, if there is one, is that the young protagonists are all intensely absorbed in the action while the chorus of middle-aged professors, who can't see that there is any action, are all excruciated with boredom. One of these protagonists is me – though it's really too dynamic a word. I'm more of a passive Chekhovian particle waiting on events, definitely not busy and definitely not ambitious. Another is the second daughter of an Osaka bank official, the one who had come furthest to be there – a student of our literature, not of hers, one who had made herself and gave every sign of having become more free from her distant origins than many of the others. Suddenly, she becomes interesting and one night the story starts.

One last excavation, because we are not just ourselves but all the history that goes to make us too. In me it's simple: it was a long family history of blank pages, centuries of stay-at-home nothingness in a small and un-noteworthy nation that finally revolted and created a quirk, a bias in the wood that led me firmly in Tomoko's direction. It takes the simple form of a preference for the strange over the familiar, for the foreign rather than the local and is so deeply rooted, so normal for me that it was a long time before I realised that other people's internal lives are organised along altogether different lines. The chief symptom is an incomprehension of racism, and a dangerous naivety with regard to its power. Tomoko sees this in me, though only in terms that make sense in her world; within weeks I am diagnosed over a cup of coffee as suffering from 'Madame Butterfly syndrome'. It's an astute remark, a little too simplistic, just a little unfair, but not wholly wrong. It's a warning too – though in those days I was still deafened by optimism. There are no doubt different readings of the story she refers to, but amongst them, surely, is that one should only love at home. I reject that still, whatever the price that's been paid for ignoring it.

And Tomoko's prehistory, the irresistible press-moulding of events, of sheer mischance that made her what she is? It's fundamental – the loss of her mother at such an early age that she could have no memory of her. It's an absence that becomes a domineering and jealous vacuum which smothers her chances of happiness one by one. The absence is memorialised every year on the day it started, unsendable letters are written to it, its old-fashioned cotton-print dress is worn when Tomoko reaches the age at which her mother died. The scientists of the mind have a phrase for this, but it's not the right one. The right one has more to do with the first lessons in love not being learned, about the sort of damage that can never be repaired.

Oh, and one other thing, of course, the one that is too obvious to mention, the one she hadn't really escaped after all. Japan.

*

So that is how it started and here is how it ends, alone in a silent, toy-strewn house in Fife in the summer of 2003. I have been searching the place and have become aware, loss by loss, just what a meticulous and thorough burglary has been committed. It's no surprise that the bank statements have gone, and one could hardly object to this any more than to an opponent's winning stroke. Birth certificates are missing too, and photographs, which surely goes beyond the strictly necessary. Then I know what I must find, and I turn the place upside down, going through it all with a breathless violence as if in a mad scene from an opera or an old play. Finally I come across the right box, but it is empty too – of a lock of Makoto's infant hair, of the two tiny hospital security bracelets and of the ultrasound picture of Satomi before he was born. The image you saw just a few pages back is someone else's child.

I am lying on a white sofa in a room full of light, waiting for the police. It is not a room I believe in any more. I don't believe in the table, the windows, the silence. I don't believe in the facts I know to be true. I don't believe, and will not for many months, that there is a single car that drives down my street which is not bringing my children back to me. I don't believe the telephone, but eventually get up to answer it all the same. It's a voice I don't know, a woman, and I am still certain she is about to tell me something of great importance when I hear her ask if the sofa is still available. I hesitate, I lie. I return to the sofa in question. I sit on it, slump on it prostrate, reach for the local paper on the table and turn to the classifieds where I find, not without a certain grim admiration, the contents of my house advertised for sale.

4 *Protect and survive*

What do you do the day after you discover your children have been taken to the other side of the world, the first day of that new and violently changed life in which you are likely never to see them again? What's the procedure, who do you call? One is the citizen of an advanced liberal democracy and has paid one's taxes – now that catastrophe has struck it goes without saying that a well-oiled and effective and highly professional procedure will swing into action. After all, people don't just disappear without any questions being asked. At the very least, someone will insist on digging over the garden, just to be on the safe side.

Whatever's going to happen, it must be started with a telephone call and this is a terrifying barrier. I can see myself, six or seven years in the past, pacing endlessly in a large open kitchen. There are windows all down one side and early summer light floods in from across the garden. Collared doves commute to and from their nest under the eaves. Satomi's drawings are stuck to the fridge door – a night scene of solid, expressionist black and another of coloured stick figures around a bonfire, arms raised in excitement as they look up at the fireworks exploding above them. I suppose they must have been there since the previous November. Beside the fridge is the telephone and beside the telephone, the directory open at the letter P. How do you make such a call, what are the first words? Worse still is the primitive, magical conviction that so long as you don't tell anyone it isn't really true. The telephone call cuts off this last hope – making the call drags the unbelievable situation out into the light, it finally crosses that line at which I have to accept this isn't a nightmare, that I am not ever going to wake up.

I need a human voice to distract me and the radio is playing quietly as I walk up and down. I check to see what it must have been about and find that the news that day was the announcement of a parliamentary inquiry into the Iraq War and some nonsense from the President of the United States about progress in the Middle East peace process. To this familiar background music I pace for an hour, maybe more, before the necessary crisis arrives and I lunge at the phone. A woman answers. I explain. She laughs. I don't want to exaggerate – she didn't find the situation particularly amusing, but with a single, dismissive laugh she certainly conveyed that she found my curt, possibly over-controlled opening sentences impossible to believe. Looking back, I try to make allowances; this is Fife, after all, and I'm not talking about livestock straying on to the road or the weekly fracas outside the Central Bar. Perhaps it was just the occurrence of the words 'abduction' and 'Japan' in the same phrase that took her by surprise. To be fair to her, she is hardly likely to have received a similar call before. I try again more slowly and with a little more detail, but find that I still have to press on through her scepticism and reluctance until she decides that the easiest way to get rid of me is to send someone out and make it their problem instead.

Two hours later the doorbell rings and I answer it to discover that the man selected to deal with this task is not a real police officer at all, but a character who clearly makes his living as a lookalike for Chief Wiggum from *The Simpsons*. He looks down at his notebook, already having forgotten my name during the long walk from his car.

'Mr Galbraith?'

Admittedly, it was a warm day, but even so the effort of climbing the three steps from the front path has exhausted him to an alarming degree. He is breathless and sweating freely – he removes his cap and wipes his forehead with the back of his hand in precisely the manner of his animated caricature. I open the other half of the double doors and he turns sideways to manoeuvre himself into the house, club, pepper spray, handcuffs, keys swinging and jangling from his belt. If this man has caught any criminals recently, it certainly wasn't on foot. We go into the breakfast room and he looks about the place. It is large, clean, orderly, gratingly unafford able. It's not what he's used to and he gives a little nod; he makes that noise and gesture people use when they've just understood something, when they've 'got the picture'. His radio squawks, but he ignores it.

'I've checked the address,' he tells me. 'No call-outs. No record here.'

By which he means, I assume, that he has satisfied himself that I am not a wife-beater, and that the whole incomprehensible business can soon be wrapped up.

We sit at the table as I recount the events of the last few days. He makes no notes of what I'm telling him and frequently signals his lack of interest, looking around the room, commenting on the passage of a train beyond the garden boundary. A strange dissociative state settles on me, one which will become normal over the months ahead. I believe I am talking, all the evidence points in that direction except for one thing – the person I am talking to clearly hears nothing. I have been shut into a parallel, soundproofed world from which it is impossible to send a message back to the one I have just left. This is the essential quality of the catastrophic moment, passing the point beyond which you can never be wholly understood, except by those few who have been there with you.

The Wiggum impersonator sighs with such a self-absorbed melancholy that I think he is about to start telling me about his problems – his wife, his feet, his beef with the pension scheme. How do I communicate with this man?

'Look, this is illegal, she's broken the law. What are you going to do about it?'

I point out the textbook on the table, I give him chapter and verse – the ancient common law offence of child-stealing, the 1984 Child Abduction Act. He looks away from me resentfully as I begin to sound like one of his superiors back at the station, and I guess he must often have had to listen to their disappointment. He shrugs and tells me 'There's a lot of laws – but what can you do?'

I ask him to find out if my children were removed through a Scottish or an English airport and explain the legal technicality that makes this important. This sounds like work, so he puts on a regretful expression and shakes his head.

'No can do.'

'I'm sorry?'

'That would be confidential.'

'Confidential? My children have been spirited out of the country – how can it be confidential? I'm their father – confidential from me?'

And so he does his Data Protection Act thing – the one law he does claim to know about – telling me that even if he could find out he would not be allowed to tell me. There's a practised air about this and I get a strong impression that the Data Protection Act is his favourite routine and that on a busy day he might quote it three, maybe four times. I wave the mail redirection notice at him.

'I've got an address but it's just a hotel – they'll only be there for a few days and then I'll lose them. The police could visit, social services maybe – for a welfare report, just to tell me how they are.'

He looks doubtful, irritated by my persistence. Japan is not real to this man and neither are my children.

'It would take an Interpol request.'

'Good – you'll arrange it?'

He shakes his head again.

'My boss wouldn't like it. It costs, you see – and the budgets we have these days, well . . .'

He trails off before struggling to his feet. As he turns to leave he says what has been on his mind the whole time, speaking not only for himself but for a wider society that has come to hold the idea of fatherhood so cheaply that it no longer seems possible to commit a crime against it.

'They're with their mum,' he tells me. 'They'll be all right.'

He's heard this before and repeats it. No thought is required, the idea is in the air and one picks it up effortlessly, like an infection. This is culture, and in the end culture always trumps the law.

I watch him as he puffs down the path towards early retirement and the relief of not having to deal with people like me any more. And no, he never did spare a glance for the flower beds and the possibility of freshly turned earth, or signs of a recent disturbance around the patio paving slabs. This is, after all, a country where people just vanish.

I am so shocked by this encounter that it takes some time for me to gather my thoughts. For a while I'm not even sure which of these two colliding realities is the right one. Could it really be true that the destruction of a whole future life of reasonable hopes and expectations is not such a notable event after all? Could it be that this is the sort of thing on which the law should be passive, voluntarily impotent – even when that destruction is not wrought by ghastly accident, but by a deliberate and reversible action? Perhaps I was not seeing things clearly. Perhaps all that had happened was that I and my children had lost in a game and there were no real issues of justice at all. I thought also of Constable Wiggum's parting remark. Had society drifted into accepting an unchallengeable female sovereignty over children which it was pointless to rail against? Looking back, it seems to me now that the police view of society was both more accurate and amoral than my own, and I was naive to be so surprised. Put another way – the police officer was of society, while I was and remain against it.

I email the local station using my best pseudo-legal style – that blend of arrogance, controlled outrage and threatening jargon which solicitors deploy when demanding money with menaces or issuing final threats of eviction to hapless tenants. Within a couple of days an inspector calls; on the telephone at least. He isn't interested in my problem either, but he is interested in whether I can cause any problems for him.

'Do you wish to make a complaint against the police?'

Those were the words, but the meaning was all in the tone. This was an offer I was definitely supposed to refuse. How best to play the cards I didn't have?

'That depends on what you do next.'

What he does next is ask me what I do for a living – a clumsy irrelevance that reveals just how successful my email had been in spooking him. By ventriloquising the style of the legal profession I had puffed myself up into something more bloated, prickly and toxic than I really was. Could I be a bump on the road to Chief Inspector? For two seconds I consider leading him further along this path, going the whole hog, how I eat police inspectors for breakfast, how the last one who crossed me was busted all the way back down to traffic patrol, how if he knew what was good for him he would . . . etc. etc. It's what fear and powerlessness does to us, making us loud and unconvincing and, in our desperation, even easier to ignore. I would have had no compunction in lying to him – I just couldn't have kept it up for long. Miserably, I tell him the truth and in doing so stumble on the one thing that will work.

'I'm a writer.'

There's a long, calculating pause and then, before brusquely hanging up, he says 'I'll send someone else.'

It's a better result than I expected and it puzzles me until

I realise that when I spoke the word 'writer' the Inspector heard 'journalist', or perhaps even 'press'. It's an early lesson in one of the most consistent dynamics of the child abduction drama: it's not the facts that motivate the authorities, it's the publicity about the facts. If you want to play the starring role in your own Lindbergh sensation, you have to do it very publicly.

A young police constable turns up and takes a lengthy statement. He is courteous and thorough and only once accuses me of lying, and even then he has a diplomatic way of phrasing it. He says he'll ask around and pass a report up the line. I see him out and wonder, as he drives away, what the spectators must make of all this. The house is part of a tight, introspective circle of buildings, the sort of place where we would all say how shocked we were by the next-door murder, though in truth we would be more excited, vivified, and not half as surprised as we pretended. And now it's from my driveway that the police cars come and go – the man helping the police with their inquiries, the woman and children vanished, the preconceptions shepherded by an uncharitable media. What on earth do they think is going on? I realise also that they must have seen the taxi called, the suitcases being loaded in the back, and my children too. As several sizeable items of furniture have also gone, typically the more Japanese in style, there can have been no subtlety about it – there must have been a bloody removal van. These people must know something about the abduction of my children that I don't: the day, the time, Tomoko's calm demeanour as she supervised the loading before slamming shut the taxi door and saying 'Airport, please'. I never ask and they never volunteer. We all agree, though probably for different reasons, that the whole thing is unspeakable.

A small, appeasing investigation is undertaken by the police which includes questioning the head teacher of Satomi's school. Within a few days I speak to her myself, the woman who obligingly released Satomi from school before the end of term on the strength of a note without my signature, the woman who never thought to pick up the phone for a word of confirmation from a child's father. By the time I get to her I sense there have already been discussions with the local department of education. I make no recriminations but she is tense, cagey and her expressions of regret have a perfunctory tone as if she is waiting for an accusation to be made. She offers to send me a copy of this note as if it is a receipt for a transaction, proof that the goods in question weren't stolen.

In truth her responsibility is very slight, but it isn't quite zero. Those who, for reasons of habit, neglect, cultural conditioning or a rooted gender politics, think it reasonable to dispose of a child on the say-so of only one parent make a choice that has, on rare occasions, disastrous consequences. It is a choice to dismiss the rights of the other parent as well as those of the child whose future is so casually determined. It's a free choice, it could have been made otherwise, there could have been a different outcome. By the end of the conversation I am not at all sure that this particular head teacher has accepted this responsibility or, if she has, that her concern extends beyond what it might mean for her if I were to take the matter any further. I certainly don't get the impression that she is about to start asking fathers for their consent to the early removal of their children from school.

From somewhere the overburdened Fife Constabulary find the few quid required to make an Interpol request to Osaka police in Japan — a costly procedure that you and I know as 'sending an email'. Tomoko, Satomi and Makoto are visited in their temporary quarters just before they move on to an address unknown; that is, unknown to me. The mother is described as 'strange' and the accommodation cramped, but neither is the case to an extent that would justify intervention. And no, they won't give me a forward address. The attitude of the Japanese authorities is predictably consistent with that of their British counterparts and their labour-saving affection for the Data Protection Act: within days I am told by officials on the opposite sides of the earth that my children are no longer my business. There is no explanation and no possibility of entering into a debate — it is a plain fact. One reads of revolutions in books but there can be few that strike the mind with such a force as this: to learn as abruptly as the turning out of a light not only that one's most vital and natural rights as a parent have come to nothing, but that one had been, all along, living in a society that barely acknowledged their existence in the first place.

A brief report is submitted to the prosecuting authorities, though I am warned in advance that this is 'for information only'. Time passes — a month, two or three? — before the arrival of a letter that consists, with the exception of the salutation and the sincerities at the end, of one and a half lines. It tells me, with no reason offered, that this matter 'is concluded' — an undeniable truth in so many ways. Perhaps it was the idea that one cannot steal one's own property that proved so neatly conclusive to the bureaucratic mind. Perhaps it was a more pragmatic decision, one that I would have accepted even then: that a criminal charge and an arrest warrant against an unextraditable absentee defendant would have been a futile gesture, and would have achieved nothing for the two children at the centre of the story. They would have been right about that – the officials I encountered were merely the current operators of a legal system that has never sought to be effective in this area, and still is not.

There was one other question that nagged at me in these early days of being a left-behind parent. I still had my children's passports, both the Japanese and the British versions. I found them where I had hidden them, useless now but precious because of the photographs they contained. The hiding place had been a good one, but Tomoko had clearly found another solution. It was obvious to me what it must have been, but I still felt I was owed an explanation for what they had done and so I telephoned the Japanese Consulate in Edinburgh.

Japan answers – not an individual, you understand, but the distilled essence of its petty officialdom. It's a young woman, instantly flustered by encountering a foreigner and with a constantly rising pitch of anxiety in her voice. It is just as well that the conversation is short. I imagine that if it had gone on any longer her mechanism would have been over-strained – a sudden nonsensical jabbering followed by a spring unleashing itself, perhaps a conflagration, the commercial secretary gallantly bounding in with fire extinguisher at the ready. Her initial approach is impressively fundamental: I am lying, I have made the whole thing up, I am a deranged time-waster and she won't tell me anything. As a brush-off technique this makes the Data Protection Act positively caring by comparison. She doesn't sound persuadable. Could I speak to someone else? No. To the Consul perhaps? Out of the question. Might I know his name so that I could write to him? No. Is his name a secret? Yes.

Happily for me, there has been an appalling security breakdown and the Consul's name appears on the front page of the website. I write to him. He ignores me. I send the same letter again, recorded delivery. He directs a minor functionary to reply, explaining that as I am almost certainly an impostor he hopes I will understand that it would be quite impossible for them to communicate with me at all. I write again, this time enclosing copies of my children's Japanese passports, solemn documents covered in the language and symbolism of the state the Consul and his staff are paid to serve — the old-style kanji characters on the front, the golden imperial chrysanthemum, and the pages inside with their Mount Fuji watermarks. This is the epistolary equivalent of playing the national anthem at full blast. They snap to attention and confess. Yes, they did it: they issued the passports that got my children out of the country. But no, they will not explain why they produced duplicate passports for two British-Japanese children who already had valid Japanese passports in issue. They will not say what questions they asked, or checks they made. They will not say why they did not think it reasonable to obtain the consent of both parents. They will not say if they understand what they have done, what the consequences are, or whether they care. All this is none of my business. An authentic, official detail is added

— it's the real purpose of the letter, the one point they wish to get clear. The passports I hold are no longer the real ones — they have been cancelled. Only the duplicates are the real ones now, the ones that did the damage.

Time passes. There are things you can't be told about scenes, internal and external, known only to those who have experienced them, incommunicable to those who have not. Happiness writes white, they say. But misery has its literature too — an equally illegible black. These are the limits of words and I shall not attempt the impossible. There is a sense of deep change, not only in my circumstances but in my identity too, my self. I am being pulled away from the old tribe and forcibly joined to the new: my people now, the only ones who know what this is. I bear new marks. I begin the process by which I will come to accept new and unfamiliar beliefs. Blow by blow, I am beaten into a new shape.

One fine day I sit on the steps that lead out to the garden. The potentilla is flowering, the fuchsia in bud. Sweet pea clambers up canes against a background of uncut grass, as offensive to my neighbours as hair on a young man's collar. The doves are busy tending to their growing family whose downy heads now poke prominently above the nest. Before the summer ends one will fledge while the other, differently abled, will flutter about the garden until vanishing one night into a fox's stomach, a small patch of feathers marking the spot where its story ended. Next year both eggs will fail to hatch, the year after a chick falls from the nest. I replace it, squeamishly gloved, but it dies anyway. The parents warm its corpse for three days before abandoning the project for another season. Here and there in the thickening undergrowth my eye picks out the brightness of unnatural colours – a small blue bucket shaped like a castle with four corner turrets and a portcullis entrance, a scarlet plastic crab, a toy ambulance canted over against a clod of earth, the word EMERGENCY printed in green on its white flank. I review the events of the last weeks. I see a pattern and begin to follow it – the nervous dismissiveness of the police receptionist and the open incredulity of her colleague in the Japanese Consulate, the coldness of the head teacher, the idleness of the police officer justified by a reference to the abductor's gender. Female voices dominate and I doubt that I had been able to make myself understood by any of them. It seemed that on this subject, the subject of a father and his children, I had almost literally lost my voice. And so a question began to form, more and more insistently: had I lost my voice recently, or had it been weakening for years through a process I had been too complacent to notice?

*

So much for one small case in a growing problem. What should happen, what happens elsewhere, what would happen in a better world?

It may not be possible in the United Kingdom to interest a police officer in the disappearance of your children – or at least, not where the other parent is involved – but that doesn't mean there is no procedure at all. There most certainly is. The procedure is user-friendly and easy to understand: you contact the Foreign Office and they send you a leaflet. I already knew this leaflet well, or its 2003 version at any rate, and from an early stage it had become confused in my mind with that most notorious of all post-war British government pamphlets, *Protect and Survive*. Older readers may know about its supposed contents – most likely gleaned from countless stand-up comedy routines of the early 1980s when Cold War fears were still dominant in popular culture. It purported to tell the British population how to survive a nuclear attack and offered such handy hints as whitewashing the insides of your windows or, depending on who you listened to, fashioning a hat from cooking foil to fend off the more irritating effects of radioactive fallout. When the Foreign Office's leaflet on parental child abduction hits the mat the connection, fanciful at first sight, is all too easy to make. In one sense the analogy is precise – the political purpose of the two documents is to suggest that the government is both competent and diligent in its efforts to make a difference when it is, in fact, neither. The child abduction leaflet is small as well as unhelpful. All the same, if one had sufficient origami skills perhaps it would be possible to work up some piece of protective headgear and wear it as one sits cross legged under the kitchen table waiting for things to improve.

I am being unfair. Apart from listing what the British government will not do for its citizens in these circumstances, the leaflet does contain one worthwhile piece of information – a pointer to the central international legal instrument in the parental child abduction scene. It doesn't work very well anywhere, and in much of the world it doesn't work at all, but it's pretty much all there is. It dates from 1980 and is called The Hague Convention on the Civil Aspects of International Child Abduction. It is a backwater of the new and optimistic legal dispensation that began around 1945 and has had as one of its most consistent themes the attempt to reach across national and jurisdictional boundaries and offer some remedy for the injustices, or crimes, committed behind these high, protecting walls. In a wider context it can be seen as part of the project to deal with the harsh consequences of globalisation, the harm that inevitably arises as the species gropes its way towards a single society while retaining the home-loving minds of villagers and tribesmen.

The Convention is a late response to a problem that was already a hundred years old when it was drawn up. It would be arbitrary to select a particular case as the start of the modern era in parental child abductions, but the Neil case of 1873 has all the required elements – at least one parent irreconcilable with a painful court judgment, or fearing what a future judgment might bring, a sheltering alternative jurisdiction into which they can flee and the material and technical wherewithal to make it happen. On the failure of his marriage, the wealthy Mr Neil was granted custody of one daughter, but not the other. Both children were living with their mother in Williamstown when he snatched them and, in the speculation of the *New York Times*, transported them to Europe where the laws of the day could not reach. Lacking the advantage of the automobile, he hired a 'fast livery team' – presumably to head straight to the docks where the new technology of the transatlantic steamship was waiting to complete the plan. Today it is the taxicab to the airport and the budget flights, booked online. The fact that the first legal response to this issue coincides with the growth of cheap air travel is really no coincidence at all – it merely marks the point at which it became unignorable.

The Convention declares its aims in the opening article: to secure the prompt return of wrongfully removed children and to secure rights of custody and access across the borders of the signatory states. For thirty years the eye of the left-behind parent has fallen on Article 1 with a renewed hope, and in a great many cases that hope has been short-lived.

The Convention replaced either an absence of law or a chaos of individual and ill-defined procedures by which the dispossessed in one country struggled to be heard in the courts of other, often very different countries. Hearings would get bogged down in the merits of individual cases and would routinely deteriorate into cross-cultural shouting matches in which even arguments about climate and cuisine would be deployed as well as the usual hands-down winners of ethnicity, nation and faith. These were little more than re-enactments of the original breakdown of the relationship and always played into the hands of the abductor, who could add to their massive home advantage the cultural sympathies of their home judiciary. The resources of the pursuer would be quickly depleted, imposing on them the loss of their financial security as well as their children. Before long an intolerable dilemma would often arise – whether to impoverish oneself by persisting with futile litigation or to make another choice which, however rational, must always strike the bereft parent as an abandonment and is liable to be portrayed by the abductor as acquiescence.

The Hague Abduction Convention seeks to short-circuit these difficulties by requiring every signatory to agree that parents in troubled families should not obtain unfair advantages over each other by skipping from one jurisdiction to another. Its central principle is that abducted children should be returned to their country of habitual residence where parental skirmishing can continue in the domestic courts, if that is what the parents wish. The procedure is led by a purpose-built 'Central Authority' in each country, relieving the left-behind parent of the burden of cost, and is supposed to focus on whether the disputed child was wrongfully removed from the original country or not. If the answer to this question is 'yes' an order should be made for the return of the child and that order should be promptly enforced. What could possibly go wrong?

Sadly, the law has long been adept at frustrating the ends of justice and the operation of the Convention illustrates this as well as any international instrument. In several jurisdictions orders for return are not immediately enforceable, in others appeals are entertained, undermining the very idea of a simple summary procedure. Endless debates are possible about the precise definitions of custody rights and wrongful removal, points often being submitted in bad faith with the intention of stringing out the process. The courts of some countries have never had the discipline to keep out of the merits of individual cases and this, coupled with a lethal get-out clause allowing the return of children to be refused if it cuts across undefined 'fundamental principles', allows contending parties to go back to their cross-cultural bickering as predictably as dogs to their vomit. A return can also be refused if abducted children are judged to have become settled in their new environment after a period of one year. While practical at first sight, one predictable consequence of this has been to turn proceedings into a game played against the clock. The abductor can easily creep up on final victory through a series of delays, procrastinations and open non-co-operation while the left-behind parent can only look on from abroad as the prospect of restoration leaks away month by month. If a return order is issued and appeals and other delaying tactics are exhausted, the self-confident abductor may still have little to fear. The presumption against assertive enforcement measures is deeply rooted and the use of contempt of court procedures to pressurise reluctant defenders is almost exceptional. When the one-year winning post is passed and the settlement argument successfully deployed the Convention both fails in its purpose and can even appear to have endorsed an abduction, the continuing effects of which are now judged to be in the best interests of the resettled child. Many cases that are held out as successes for the Convention mechanisms are in fact voluntary or semi-voluntary returns by abducting parents who ran out of nerve, money or stamina, or who acted out of an exaggerated respect for their adversary, never understanding how tooth-less it is.

This is not the usual presentation of the Convention, routinely described in glowing terms by establishment praise-singers as a vindication of the very idea of inter-national civil law and as having spread a new and humane norm across much of the world. As the Convention's effect-iveness is above zero the 'better than nothing' defence can fairly be applied and as such it is also good that its feeble influ-ence should be as widespread as possible. An up-to-date list of signatories appears impressive, but this is no European Union – there are no high tests to be passed before admission, no rigorous scrutiny of how governments meet their obligations, no way of deprecating their failures, and no one is ever expelled, however delinquent. The fact that Zimbabwe and Turkmenistan are numbered among the just, as far as parental child abduction goes, says little about the club except that anyone can be a member. The habit of judges, civil servants and legal academics in expressing an unjustified confidence in the Convention's workings arises partly from an innately conservative *déformation professionelle* as well as from a sincere desire to support the fragile credibility of international law itself. From an outsider's point of view, much that is passed off as international law has neither the precision nor the enforceability to justify the word 'law' at all. A sizeable part of it consists of liberal western wish-fulfilment. Its pieties are an atheist's prayer – the required words are spoken, the required gestures enacted by the publicly faithful, despite knowing there is really nothing there, that no miracles are to be expected.

Defenders of the Convention admit its weaknesses but seek either to diminish or conceal their scale. Information about its practical effectiveness has often not been collected and its advocates remain strikingly coy about hard figures for the return of actual children. Some external pressure is typically needed and a UK ministerial answer to a written parliamentary question tabled in 1998 shows what it is they are so keen to hide: applications received in the previous year regarding abductions to France 16, judicial returns 1; applications regarding Spain 13, judicial returns 1; applications regarding Germany 16, judicial returns 1. That's a 93 per cent failure rate even between major European jurisdictions.

Larger numbers of these cases are said to have been resolved by 'other means', which might suggest that there are other, more promising avenues to pursue until one realises that 'resolution' can include the left-behind parent simply giving up in exhaustion or despair. This is resolution only for the abductor.

Over its lifetime the Convention has no doubt achieved a significant number of returns that would not otherwise have happened. Nevertheless, it remains largely disappointing and continues to fall far short of its aims. The final clause of Article 7 that obliges signatory countries to work continually to eliminate any obstacles to its effectiveness is, without question, the most flagrantly dishonoured part of the whole document. This has categorically not happened and that the agreement should remain so weak after thirty years of operation cannot plausibly be passed off as a misfortune. It is blameworthy.

Lined up against the Convention and its good intentions is the divisive wedge of cultural differences, deep seated gender norms, the visceral desire to hold rather than surrender one's children and the mutual loathing and distrust of warring parents. These are powerful enemies and its relative failure in the face of such opposition should be no great surprise. On the cultural front a glance down the list of signatory states is exactly what one would expect. The Islamic world, with only a few exceptions, continues to reject the Convention's humane and compromising embrace. In China, its microscopic footprint does not extend beyond Hong Kong and the casinos of Macau where it persists as a legacy of British and Portuguese rule. India will have none of it. Viewed from these locations it is, like much of international law, unconvincing as a culturally neutral instrument. There's something too obvious about the way international law emanates from the West – intellectually, historically, even physically – for it to be easy for the non-western world to co-operate with its foreign reasonableness, the abrasive superiority of its values. It is hardly unexpected that Japan should lead these holdouts, maintaining a unique status as the only major and fully developed country to continue to reject the provisions of the Child Abduction Convention. The government of Japan has been considering the Convention for many years. Occasionally, under a little gentle diplomatic pressure – usually from the United States – it will consider it more urgently. In a recent change of position, it now proposes to submit a bill on the subject to the Diet later in 2011. The practical reality remains that no abducted child has ever been recovered from Japan as a result of legal proceedings and it remains highly doubtful that this will change in the foreseeable future.

I knew this while waiting on the station platform for the car that never came. I knew it while levering open a window to climb into my own home. My interest in the Hague International Child Abduction Convention has always been theoretical.

*

It is July 2003, or maybe August by now – it doesn't matter. I find a website for the temporary accommodation Satomi, Makoto and their mother are using. It has a floor plan of the studio flats and from this I work out the addresses of the apartments around theirs, and the others on the floor below. I mail them pictures of my children, requests for information and an email address. Two weeks later all these envelopes come back in a neat packet bound with a rubber band – unopened, undelivered, but very efficiently returned by the Japanese Post Office. They're in a box now, a set of steadily ageing Wanted posters waiting to puzzle whoever might open them years from now.

My family moves on and all I know from this point is that they are somewhere in Japan. The British Consulate is cooling on the whole story and I feel that if I wanted advice on placing an order for ball bearings I would be getting a little more of their attention. They have Tomoko's mobile telephone number, but they won't tell me what it is. Civil servants have been known to leak the odd bit of information now and again, but not on this occasion. Perhaps it is just a wise neutrality when the female consular staff take their lead from the female abductor, then again, perhaps it isn't.

The acceptance of impotence comes slowly and only after a long rearguard action against evidence and reason. At this stage my mind and reality are in two very different places and there is an overwhelming need to make gestures. Where only futile gestures are available, futile will have to do. One by one all the required elements coalesce – a hopeless case, a still innocent faith in the law and its claimed effectiveness, less innocent convictions about the intimate connection between justice and money, a deep hurt, and the phrase 'something must be done' tolling ceaselessly inside my head. These props dress the stage and, on an appropriate cue, there enters the lawyer. This one is, if you please, a common or garden example of what must be history's most durably hated profession. Not for him the late shift at the immigrants' advice centre or heroic pro bono defences of the persecutees of the state – this man's career is not coming to a small screen near you any time soon. He is from the other, more populous side of the profession and practises in its ancient and self-honoured traditions – those that stretch all the way from the show court politicians of the Roman Republic, down through the intervening seventy generations of fee-seekers and cab-rank moralists to the distinctive species of the modern world: the celebrity divorce attorney, the class action shakedown merchant and the libel tart. I first catch sight of him rising through a trapdoor, wreathed in gory light and sulphurous fumes, precisely as Mephistopheles appeared in answer to Faust's fateful call. That, I suppose, is his defence – he is at least no ambulance chaser. I call him, and this must lead me, in all fairness, to ask what these people might do with themselves if disputatious humanity were not constantly bringing them so much business.

'Do you want a divorce?'

'I want my children.'

'Yes, but do you want a divorce?'

I make an appointment anyway.

In the full light of day he is an unprepossessing figure, the only trace left on my memory being the fact that he conducts the entire interview unaware that his jacket collar is rucked up at the back, like an untidy schoolboy. I should have been paying more attention to what he was saying but become oddly preoccupied with this imperfection to the extent that

I can hardly take my eyes off it and am constantly looking a few inches to his left, giving the impression, no doubt, that I have a squint. He presents himself as a great expert on the matter in hand with much experience in international actions. On the issue of Japan in particular he is suavely evasive but betrays no lack of confidence. As the following months gradually reveal, this is a highly misleading advertisement and by the time we part company I might just as profitably have retained him to repair my washing machine or to spay the cat or to perform any task at which he would have been entirely ineffective. I suppose he must have mentioned his fees towards the end, discreetly ushering them past me as an undertaker might whisper his charges to a victim too vulnerable or decent to haggle. I only recall following the dishevelled and dandruff-flecked collar off the premises.

There follows, at a leisurely pace, a series of inaccurate and badly drafted documents that I have to correct myself at many points. The second act is an extended and ultimately unproductive confusion over how to serve a writ in Japan. The finale is the invoice. In some ways this is an improvement as it is the first item they send me to which they have devoted their full attention and ingenuity. Despite being an initial account and the fact that nothing whatever has been achieved, it is already several pages long and an altogether desperate piece of work.

Amongst its several inventions one of the most rewarding is the pay-as-you-fail accounting system, a classic fee-boosting wheeze. This means that every time they get something wrong they are obliged to charge me even more for all the time and effort required to read my emails telling them they've got it wrong and to make the necessary corrections. This gives them a direct financial interest in low drafting standards – the more mistakes they make, the more fees they charge; the more quickly they get something right, the less profitable it is for them. For this firm, it is immensely lucrative.

Their *pièce de résistance* is the most bounteous of all: the multi-partner 'ignorance is gold' case conference. Here's how it works. There's my man, furrowing his learned brow on my behalf as he peruses some very complicated documents. He's not reading them, let's get that straight from the outset. You're reading now. It's not very difficult and it's not worth much, but this fellow is perusing and that's worth three hundred pounds an hour. After one of these hours has passed his brow remains furrowed. There's a problem. It's a rather basic one: he has no idea how to start the ball rolling by serving a writ on a prospective divorce respondent in Japan. The reason he doesn't know is that he hasn't bothered to look up the Foreign Office website where the procedure is explained. But that's by the way – this man is a skilled professional, he is a man of initiative, he will know what to do. He presses a button on the intercom.

'Deirdre, pet – I've no bloody idea what to do. Send in another partner, would you?'

A second man enters the room and the first says to him –

'I have perused all these documents, but the old magic just isn't working for me this morning. Why don't you peruse them all over again – see if you can come up with something.'

Perusal efforts are redoubled. We'll skip this bit. All you

have to notice is the hands on the clock in the background continuing to turn. After much additional perusal it's still no dice. There's only one thing to do – namely, to repeat what didn't work before. Deirdre gets the buzz for a second time.

'Deirdre – it's a crisis. The whole firm is in danger of looking incompetent. Send in another partner.'

A third man enters. Perusal escalates to a hitherto unheard-of intensity. Will they all make it? It's touch and go. After a further substantial period there's still no joy. They collapse – shattered, exhausted, all perused out. The third man shrugs his shoulders and speaks.

'Search me, cock. I'm no more in the loop on this one than you are. Why did you tell the guy you could handle it if you couldn't?'

There's an extended, but still billable, silence before the tension breaks and they all burst out laughing. The third man speaks again.

'I can't help noticing,' he says, 'that there are three people in this room. Three, so to speak, members of the same trade assembled together. That's a powerful heap of legal expertise and it seems to me it would only be fair to triple-charge the client.'

His colleagues agree – and that is how the multi-partner 'ignorance is gold' case conference works.

At the bottom of this invoice is a number, a demand that anyone who had not long since forgotten the difference between ethics and professional ethics would have been ashamed to present – but there it is all the same. I have care-fully preserved this document and watched as it has expanded to a rather grand status that, in truth, it doesn't really deserve. For all I know of history and its bleakest records it is this piece of paper, in its own small and private way, that now defines for me the very essence of cynicism. It is this, an Edinburgh solicitor's invoice, that taught me something new about greed. I sack them instantly, and send a cheque.

There is a postscript to this little story, or more of a damp trailing off. It happens months later – a rainy, midwinter scene by a junction at the top of the High Street in the heart of Edinburgh's old town. Everything is grey, or black. The darkest architectural smear is a spiky, threatening cathedral just down the road. On the other side, past the traffic lights and a slime-green statue said to resemble David Hume, is the High Court of Justiciary. It is for this that a small, barely noticeable protest has positioned itself amid the flow. I must have been coming north from the library, absorbed in solving a novelist's problem. I am almost past before I catch sight of them and, specifically, the most bedraggled of these threats to the established order and the placard he is holding. It bears a name that lights up for me, the name of the law firm that must not be mentioned. I take a leaflet and see that it calls lawyers crooks, frauds and thieves, that it alleges a conspiracy against the little man. The language is sincere and no doubt accurately conveys the protesters' sense of injustice, of outrage. They believe every word of it, but it is not the language of power. It is intemperate and altogether too candid; not even I am persuaded. The folks that come and go from the High Court of Justiciary do not look up. The three leafleteers have no rights of audience.

I engage the placard-bearer in conversation, telling him that I am a fellow sufferer and realising only too late that I have stumbled across the Ancient Mariner of legal complaint. He is interested in his story, not mine, and he will have his way. It's a complex and arid affair, the details defeating even the teller, who reverses over several passages in his determination to get them right – the entanglement of a commercial tenancy, a conflict of interest and a wrecked business. His life has become the presentation of his case. I lose interest at an early stage, though there doesn't seem to be any way I can get this across to him. Besides, as a loser of children rather than money I quickly decide that I massively outpoint him – loss can be such a competitive business.

The man draws breath before elaborating on his ninth point and I see my chance, nipping in with a breezy and meaningless 'Good luck, friend', before turning abruptly and making my escape. From a seven-year distance I look back at him, colourless, translucent, dissolving in the endless rain like his placard, not wholly real, the sort of character one is always coming across in the underworld, a warning of how not to be if one is to hold on to a place amongst the living.

*

There are other ways of monetising injustice. The law does not yet have a perfect monopoly – violence and deception still have their share of the market and can often be more effective, as well as less costly. International child abduction is no exception to this rule and precisely because it is an area of such legal failure it is unsurprising that there are alternative service providers. Indeed, the law has often encouraged vigorous self-help, endorsing the status of whoever has physical hold of a child. The most striking early illustration involved the redoubtable Mrs McQuiston of New York in the 1870s. Several weeks after the end of her relationship with Mr McQuiston, this man returned to break down her door and snatch what he claimed was his infant son from the cradle. Happily, Mrs McQuiston was possessed of superhero powers and immediately leapt from a second floor window and gave chase so effectively that all parties ended up in the police court. Here McQuiston explained that he was only acting for the best on the grounds that the mother had taken up with a Negro waiter. Mrs McQuiston replied compellingly that as she had only met the abductor two weeks before the boy was born, he had no paternal interest in the matter whatever. The judge waved all this away and relied instead on the sacredness of property.

'You have the boy,' he said to Mr McQuiston. 'Keep him until the law says otherwise.'

The now legally approved abductor left the court immediately with his prize and hailed a cab. It was at this point that Mrs McQuiston revealed impressive intellectual as well as physical powers, grasping at once the essential passivity of the law and that what was required was action. She ran outside and caught up with the cab then leapt on to the platform, punching McQuiston in the face and pulling the child from his arms before making off with, it is plausibly reported, a scream of triumph. It was not long, however, until the law caught up with her and she found herself before the same judge for a second time. She had learned her lessons quickly and was ready for him.

'What is law for one parent ought to be law for the other,' she told the judge. 'I stand here just exactly as he stood a few moments ago. Now give him the law as you gave it to me . . . I could not see the justice then, but I can now.'

The judge said what, in all probability, he always said on these occasions.

'You have the boy. Keep him until the law says otherwise.'

The McQuiston case was a speeded-up, Keystone Kops production of a parental abduction and counter-abduction with the law staying firmly to one side as commentator and fatalistic Greek chorus. For all the additional complexity and pretension it has gained over the intervening hundred and forty years, the law's attitude has not fundamentally changed. The message is clear: what works best against parental child abduction is another abduction.

Around the edges of the abduction scene there are a few colourful characters who offer precisely this sort of specialised service. The dream scenario they hold out – of effectiveness where nothing else is effective, of miraculously resurrecting a dead parenthood – is one that bulks large in the mind of anyone who has faced these problems. They include a predictable number of frauds and charlatans and often describe themselves as former members of elite units of the armed forces. Sometimes this is fantasy, but occasionally it is true and there are verifiable cases where these people have delivered what they promised – a fact that puts them pretty close to the head of the queue when it comes to ethical

standards in this area. I sidle up to the most credible in one of
cyberspace's dingier basement bars and tell him my problem.
Before long news gets around and I am in touch with several
of these unusual mercenaries. One is of the opinion that
anything is possible, but is keen to talk budget first: he envis-
ages some regrettable upfront expenses and I worry that he's
beginning to sound like a defrocked lawyer. Another is in
quite a different situation – having lost his own child in
similar circumstances he proposes a co-partnership involving
snatching people off the streets of Osaka with a van. My two
boys can be added to the pickup list. He tells me he's worked
it all out, though it gets a bit hazy after the van thing. This
sure-to-work non-plan is conveyed in spiky, disordered, over-
agitated prose that suggests a diagnosable detachment from
reality and that the writer is probably the sort of person you
wouldn't want near your children at any price. It forces me to
recognise that the whole idea of counter-abduction involves
a peculiarly modern judgement of Solomon: what are the
risks, could it all go hideously wrong, would it make things
worse, is it an equally offensive mirror image of the original
crime?

The last mercenary – who is the real ex-soldier – makes
the reasonable point that these things tend to work best
where there are poorly monitored land borders and readily
bribable officials. Japan ticks neither box – how serious am I?
He claims to have been there recently and doesn't like the
high visibility of the police or the number of security and
traffic-flow cameras. I pore over maps and, guessing that my
children are somewhere in the north of the vast Osaka
conurbation, get a quote for a private jet from the local Itami

airport to Seoul. I am given a very reasonable price and asked when I would like to book it. My contact gets back to me and says he doesn't like airports but has access, in an unexplained way, to a fast boat moored in Osaka Bay. This new image fills my daydreaming mind – a sleek white arrow bounding over the Korea Strait, the Japan coastguard cutter and its loudhailer demands to stop receding into the distance. There are two problems with this. The first is that between Osaka and Korea is, well, Japan itself, which suggests that my abductor for hire is planning on going a very long way around or hasn't looked at a map lately. The other is more fundamental – it's the farcical Bond-movie soundtrack I can never wholly suppress whenever I conjure a vision of this boat. In the end I can't believe in any of it and do nothing.

Looking back, I can't say this was the wrong decision. I knew that no one had ever recovered an abducted child from Japan before and there were no special reasons why I should be the first to succeed. I knew also that at least one short prison sentence has been served by someone who tried. But when self-reproach is needed – and it does seem, at times, to be a positive need – this is the first and best instrument that comes to hand: that in the defining moment of crisis I turned out to be made of far inferior stuff to the Mrs McQuistons of this world.

*

More rationally, I could tell myself that as I did not know where my children were, the *Mission Impossible* team and even the man with the van would all have been for nothing and were no more than therapeutic fantasies. Days pass like this, weeks, months. The first childless Christmas must be endured. I am trapped underwater and emerge in early January, gasping, a little surprised still to be there and already with a fearful eye on the next one. I am supposed to be writing a novel. A contract has been signed and must be obeyed. The piece was meretricious in the first place but now, being ground out in an empty house, is spectacularly pointless.

At the supermarket I have to move my car, having habitually taken up one of the privileged parent-with-child places near the entrance. When I come out, I see the yellow diamond that proclaims CHILD ON BOARD still stuck to the back window, and the issue of when to remove it fully occupies my mind. Each additional day of absence weighs more heavily. My children have been removed from my life as completely as by a literal death – but it's a limbo existence where there can be no mourning so long as restoration of the lost is at once possible and impossible.

It is early 2004. At the end of the month the Hutton Report into the death of the former UN Iraq weapons inspector David Kelly is published. The liars are exonerated, while those who tried to speak the truth are criticised and, in some cases, compelled to resign – it is widely recognised as a new low in British public life. This is the radio wallpaper as I plug away at a novel of the low, dishonest 1930s. The air is thick with lies, they have become the principal medium of British politics in a way quite new and unfamiliar to anyone of a peacetime generation. One would swear that one could smell them, drifting over everything from some stinking municipal facility just below the horizon.

'See you Thursday. Have fun.'

The words are so real I turn to confront the speaker. But it's only me, there again on the station platform, waiting for the red car that never comes. Public and private converge in a neat, reinforcing fit. I find myself drawing up an account of the price I've paid for not lying – the CVs not embellished, the odious patrons not flattered, the sharp truth not suppressed whenever in the company of another influential moral defective. It's quite a bill. At school I escaped a caning and suspension by lying. The headmaster demanded I look him in the eye and tell him the truth. I looked him in the eye and told him a beautiful, barefaced and magnificently effective lie. I made him believe what I wanted him to believe, I made him do what I wanted him to do. It is my only entirely happy memory of school, and a deep-buried lesson.

It is time to change up to the higher morality – it is time to start lying. As I can achieve nothing myself it is essential to become someone else, and as the old gender hasn't been working so well for me lately, I have to change that too. So I become Sarah, Sarah Levi in particular who knows all the right people in eighteenth-century English studies and is in a position to offer Tomoko the re-publication in a prestigious book of her only scholarly paper. That is to say, to offer her the only thing that will bump her up from being the part-time language teacher she was in Reading to being a proper lecturer in a Japanese university. This is a hand-tied fly for one very particular fish – but where to cast it? I guess that Tomoko is trying to use the last professional connection still open to her: her old university. And so I send it to their alumni office, with my respects and gratitude in advance for their help in passing it on to their former student, should they happen to know her whereabouts.

A fortnight passes. My routine is to fire up the computer at the start of each day, time-waste on the net, correspond with others involved in their own abduction stories and then squeeze out a few hundred words of fiction. I must have been giving up hope of my other character ever coming to life when I spotted something in my inbox on 28 January, 2004. I open it and read:

'Dear Sarah . . .'

In the end, it was only lying that worked.

5   *Men and women*

In the early days a comforter comes and for the sake of getting out of the house, away from the scene of it all, we repair to a nearby tourist town. The hysteria of a provincial tearoom surrounds us: chintz on all surfaces that will bear it, an excess of ruched fabric wrinkling every curtain rail, agricultural scenes, horse brasses, knick-knacks. It is impossible to imagine a meaningful sentence ever having been pronounced in such a place. Everything about it, from the whimsicality of the ornaments, through the pathology of its obsessive order to the dismaying perfection of the tea cosy – speaking, as it does, of the withering waste of life required to make it – everything signifies that suffering is not real, that because nothing matters, nothing much can ever be lost.

It occurs to me later   much later   that this may be the secret purpose of such establishments; that the more cunning in our human ecology lead others to take a seat for afternoon tea, calculating that here will be the safest and most anaesthetic place to do the deed, to finally tackle that little awkwardness which has been building for weeks, months, or decades. And so, between one sip of Earl Grey and the next, comes the unforeseen break-up, the confession, the infidelity, the revenge, the 'Oh, really Henry, you must have known that Perdita was never your daughter. And to be perfectly frank, my dear, Fluellen is only a fifty–fifty chance at best. You don't mind, do you? Not now, after all this time?'

They pay. They rise and take their coats from the rustic hooks in the hall. They observe the niceties. It is all impeccable. The bell tinkles as they open the door to leave and they go out past a display of leaflets recommending local attractions. One might think that nothing had happened at all.

So it was, in a way, on this occasion. Against the uninterrupted background of chinking crockery and talk of the weather and who has died, I hear the words, 'You could never have brought them up on your own.' It takes a second or two before I understand that this sentence refers to my children, and to me, their father who has lived with them almost every day of their six- and four-year-old lives and played a sizeable part in keeping them fed, washed, clothed, entertained, educated and funded until all these activities were so recently and abruptly ended. As I grasp it, this extraordinary statement falls on me like a physical blow. I edge sideways to find the hard anchor of the table beneath the starched cloth. It is an oddly dislocating moment – all the more so because no one else has reacted. It is as if someone has started shouting obscenities from the back row of the church and only I can hear them. Is everyone else mad, or am I? I can't tell, but one thing is for sure – we can't all be thinking straight; some of us must have got this whole situation horribly wrong.

The speaker chatters on in innocent oblivion and I come to understand that I have not heard her views, but those of a generation, a class, and above all a gender. This is a ready-made opinion, put together by other people long ago and now taken down from the rack and used, thoughtlessly, for what seemed to be the right occasion. In the world of well-meaning small talk it's a partial defence, but it won't do for those who have a responsibility to think more clearly. When the same unexamined habits of mind are found in the social worker, the police officer, the Family Division judge, the politician and the journalist these people must be questioned more closely and asked to account for the choices they make and the harm that can follow.

Outside, walking to the car, I experience new and unwelcome doubts. Whose side is this person on? Is it now the loyalties and prejudices of gender that cut across all other bonds? It's an unsubtle question, an unfair one of the old 'are you with me or against me?' sort to which we are so vulnerable in times of trouble. I hear it on the radio, and it's always been a hit with flag-wavers and proselytisers, the instinctive dividers of humanity. Here it is again, tugging at me, inviting me to join in the business of taking sides, of endorsing division, widening it even, becoming a protagonist in the bitterness of modern gender politics.

*

There is always some trouble on hand between men and women. We have been long accustomed to the idea that it varies in detail only, but that in degree and in its fundamentals it is always the same, a fixed point in our lives, ordained by nature, or by nature's imagined architects and as such quite beyond our power to change. An argument between man and wife, from however ancient a work of literature, always seems fresh to us. Two and a half thousand years ago the theatregoers of Athens watched as Medea murdered her children and then, last week, five miles across town, Theresa

Riggi short-circuited her divorce proceedings by killing hers too in a flat off the Slateford Road, in an already passing sensation. 'Ah,' says one classically informed Edinburgh citizen as he folds down his newspaper to chat to another, 'there you go — nothing new under the sun.' Change in the relations between the genders was not to be expected; at least, not before those relations became political. Instead, this aspect of our lives was viewed with fatalism; largely satisfied on the part of the male, resigned on the part of the female.

A few hundred years ago humanity's most important single idea began to spread and grow in strength — namely, that by thinking about problems you can, sometimes, fix them. Ships no longer wandered quite so haphazardly on the seas, bridges and other buildings stopped falling down quite as often as they used to and people who always died of certain diseases now, as a result of less random interventions by their doctors, only mostly died of them. Perhaps the world didn't haven't to be the way it was. If you didn't like it you could change it.

People noticed that this new approach worked better than the old ways and, bit by bit, they began to pray less and think more. They shared their new enthusiasms with their friends and taught them to their children. The pace quickened. Steadily at first, and then over the last two hundred years, in an increasingly explosive drama, modernity arrived for most people in most parts of the world. There is no more exciting story, but it has one striking deficiency — that until surprisingly late on in the plot there are few if any female characters and fewer still with speaking roles. So where were the girls through these long, slow, early chapters? Did they really have nothing to contribute, or was something holding them back?

Sooner or later the question was bound to arise. That's the problem with reason – it is essentially unruly. In an era of general improvement why should progress be restricted to the sewerage system or to grinding larger telescope lenses? Why should the same rational approach not also be applied to the relations between men and women? With careful study and thought the faults in this relationship could be diagnosed and reforms proposed. A course could be plotted for improvement in those areas that touch most intimately on human happiness. Over time the forces of reaction would be worn down by evidence and the relentless superiority of rational argument.

It all sounds wonderful, and the most surprising thing is that this is pretty much what happened. Around the end of the eighteenth century the French revolutionary Declaration of the Rights of Man was rewritten with female pronouns instead of male and gender politics was born – grammatical from the outset. Before long, Mary Wollstonecraft produced, in *A Vindication of the Rights of Woman*, what is still the best candidate for a founding text of a movement that would bring about a rolling transformation in the fairness of our living arrangements over the next two centuries. Progress slackened for a while as the straight-thinkers concentrated their efforts on those other slaves, but when that was done they got back to the woman question and there was no stopping them. Through a series of landmark stages such as married women's property rights and, above all, equal voting rights, the *ancien régime* of patriarchy was weakened and then largely dissolved. Its defenders had called this system nature, but it wasn't that, it was just an idea, as subject to attack and eventual dismissal from the collective mind as any other bad idea.

By the middle of the twentieth century Rosie the Riveter had won the Second World War, and she had achieved this victory over societies where women stayed at home to give birth to armies rather than go out to work to equip them. It was an emphatic demonstration that equal rights made everyone more powerful, not just women. Countries whose national agenda in the post-war period was to catch up with the West observed this and responded to a greater or lesser extent. Without it always being realised at the time, feminist policies began to gain traction for reasons of economic pragmatism as much as fairness, and some consciously used the language of justice as a cover for expanding the workforce. Their hearts were in the wrong place, but they did the right thing anyway. Elsewhere great forward strides were achieved incidentally. MacArthur's occupation armies brought the vote to the women of Japan and the victory of communism in China brought to power a party that was deeply imbued with aspects of western political thought, rhetorically committed to equality and, from the gender point of view, reasonably even-handed in its dictatorial tendencies. Even the world's new Jewish state was compelled to leave behind its patriarchal traditions in the struggle for survival: Israel's women were needed in new roles, whatever the Torah might have to say about these upsets to the divine order. The only major world-views to put up much resistance have been Catholicism and Islam, the 'Mahometanism' defined by Wollstonecraft in 1792 as viewing women as subordinate beings and not part of the human species. These failures are not surprising as they are part of theism's general rearguard action against rationality. It is Islam that may be about to produce one of the more notable ironies in the late history of gender equality – namely, that America's war in Afghanistan, in default of any other credible justification, risks turning into a war for women's rights; the first time a literal army has taken the field for such a purpose since the days of the Amazons themselves albeit, on this occasion, by accident.

Towards the end of the twentieth century the loose ends of this process were tied up with some anti-discrimination legislation here, an equal pay act there. By the mid-1980s even women in Switzerland and Liechtenstein could vote. For the developed world at least, the rational world, the long revolution in inter-gender justice appeared largely complete.

Spikier partisans can still get heated over pay differentials, pornography or the insult of having a door held open for them by a man. While not trivial, these irritations are small beer by comparison with voting and property rights. Recent calls for the sisterhood to return to the barricades have met with a lukewarm response, and although the journey towards perfect fairness continues, the urgency has been replaced with a sense of arrival at a more or less acceptable settlement. If this is true, a very important chapter in history is drawing quietly to a close – one which, by long, slow force of argument alone has delivered more justice for more people than any other transformation in our thinking. It's understandable that we want to feel good about this, especially as it must mean that, having finally broken through to the ideal of gender equality, men and women must now be happier with each other than ever before and that their children are sharing in the benefits of these improved relationships. And yet we are not at all sure that this is actually true. Instead, we are troubled by the defining anxiety of the current period: that while everything else has advanced since 1945, the quality of our personal and family lives has, uniquely, deteriorated.

I used not to reflect much on these questions, being only vaguely aware of broad social trends measured in statistics about other people's lives. If questioned while still in this sleepy state I would have placed myself among the beneficiaries of these changes – the ample material surplus, the absurd luxury of being able to earn a living by writing literary fiction, and from this the enjoyably half-feminised existence of living at home and fully with my children, never having to ask the hired help for an update on my own family after an economically mandated absence of fifty or sixty hours a week. Briefly, I lived close to the logical endpoint of all campaigns for gender equality: a metaphorical hermaphroditism in which gender roles, in all but their irreducible core, verge on the invisible. Of course, it's hard to keep it going while still being merely human – before too long Mr or Ms Individual is going to want a bigger share of the fairness; is going to want to win.

And so the editor makes a cut and there's a new scene – a solitary figure, listless, stunned, frozen in a moment of catastrophe from which he or she can never entirely move on. It's a new stereotype: the Miss Havishams of the modern world, framed by the symbols of the life that has just been cut off. Not the mouldering wedding dress this time, or the desiccated cake feeding only the mice, but the toys, the *Ivor the Engine* video, the half-sized guitar and the smudged remains of the crayon drawing on the wall that caused such a row.

This character – for current purposes let's just call him 'I' – so, I am settling down one day for a serious wallow in this situation when a news story of early 2004 distracts me. It's a story of everyday events in the Family Division of the High Court – a distressed figure is seen leaving the premises, a man, a non-custodial parent who has finally failed to engage the law's support in his battle to see his young daughter who lives with his ex-wife. Nothing newsworthy about that. What propels this into the papers is that the judge who has just presided over this little drama has also reached the end of his tether and lets fly with a burst of rare candour. He describes the litigant's trust in the law over the preceding two years of hearings as an exercise in absolute futility and the system he represents as being scandalous, shameful and liable to forfeit public trust. He states that many of the submissions to the court from the custodial parent, the mother, he finds impossible to believe and without ever using the word he hints that she has acquired a practical immunity to the rules of perjury. He admits that the performance of the court has been 'wholly inadequate'. Feathers are ruffled, there's a bit of a debate, things move on. For all I know Mr Justice Munby was taken to one side and given some fatherly advice about the benefits of silence to his future legal career. I couldn't say if that happened, and I certainly couldn't say whether he accepted the advice or not, but he didn't repeat the performance and he's now Lord Justice Munby.

I'm wary of the interest this story has for me and assume it must relate to my new circumstances. I doubt I would even have noticed it before and suppose this is what is meant by 'consciousness raising'. I glimpse an alarming and highly undesirable future – not of a raised consciousness, but a narrowed one; the mind that used to be mine shrunk to a deaf-blind partisan for whom everyone on his side is abundantly supplied with extenuating circumstances, while all the victims on the other side get what they deserve. Any more of this and I'm going to start spontaneously coming up with slogans, or losing my sense of humour.

I warn myself not to make too much of it, but before long another example emerges, another variation on an increasingly persistent theme. Again it's a tale of things going wrong between men and women, though what attracts the journalists this time is more irony than outrage. On this occasion it's a barrister and part-time judge who is subject to false accusations of domestic abuse, is barred from certain parts of his own home by a court order obtained without his knowledge, and who must now make an appointment to see his children. One can sympathise with his reaction, while still observing a certain naivety – 'I cannot believe that someone like me is so powerless . . . I had no idea of the unfairness of the courts until I became involved with them myself.' Presumably he means involved with them as a litigant. But it's not the blunderings of the law that are so interesting here – it is merely an instrument, called in and manipulated by contestants in a pre-existing conflict. It's another comment that catches my eye, one that refers to the underlying dispute itself and seems to focus on a widespread sense of disappointment that our new and fairer society has not delivered what we had hoped for. The ex-husband and, to an extent, ex-father complains 'This is what is so hurtful about all this. I belong to a generation of men who saw their marriage as being part of a team . . . But she has behaved like an old-fashioned chauvinist, effectively saying to me "you've served your purpose, now go away".' The shock is all the greater because the phrase is so familiar — it is what men were once imagined to say to their faded partners. More widely, it hints at a basic mistake of the optimists who did not foresee that fairness might do little more than ensure a more equal distribution of cruelty.

And so others have it bad too, as consolation's evil twin often reminds us. Are these stories just straws in the wind, or evidence that the grumblers are right, that modernity means updating the unhappiness of men and women rather than diminishing it?

My thoughts take a slightly surreal turn as I decide to leave the problem for another day. I drop the newspaper, put my feet up on the unsold white sofa and drift off. I don't how long I'm out — never long enough in these early days, when only unconsciousness can give me what I need. It's the television that pulls me back up, but it's a struggle to be sure just when I'm awake again. The nonsense, the impossibility of dreams has spilled out on to the screen. So far as I can make out it's a news item about how Batman has been dealing with the challenges of retirement. He's been at the cheeseburgers and has evidently given up the gym membership, his tights wrinkling unheroically on his once athletic legs. The whole thing has been a blow to his confidence and it's sad to see him perching so anxiously on the ledge of a building, waiting to be helped down by a man on a ladder. It's only as I gain another few degrees of wakefulness that I begin to grasp the commentary. I've got it all wrong — it's an ordinary man, dressed up to look powerful precisely because he isn't. It's a very hurt man who thinks the world should pay him some attention, and because he represents others as well as himself he's right about this. He's also a man who has a sound understanding of the media — he knows just what they like; a novelty, a bit of a laugh, something simple, and they have duly turned out in numbers to take their pictures and report the story.

There's a point to it all, of course — it's a Fathers for Justice protest, part of a quirky campaign that runs through the early years of the century. It's a sort of show in multiple, slightly random parts, put on by casualties of the new way of doing things. On the whole they are treated roughly in the press, including by some people who should, perhaps, have been more alive to the historical resonances of what they're doing. This group is, after all, a society of the disenfranchised, campaigning against a gender-based injustice through the medium of the publicity stunt and as such these men qualify as the suffragettes of the early twenty-first century. Unlike their predecessors they never achieve very much and give up pretty quickly.

But that's for the future. On this occasion, early in 2004 it's enough to wake me up. I can explain the abduction of my children in terms of culture, nationalism, race and as part of the troubled personal history of an individual — but it also, on the simplest level, is something that happens between a man and a woman. Having your children suddenly vanish to the other side of the planet might seem such a rarity that it's hardly worth thinking about, but as I watched Batman clamber down towards the waiting police I understood how it was part of a bigger picture and not so special after all. Absence is absence, always absolute. My Japan is another man's worthless contact order, my ten thousand miles, his endlessly adjourned court hearing.

*

How's that other woman in my life — Sarah Levi, the one who doesn't exist? Tomoko is getting on well with her and is enthusiastic about her publishing proposal. She sends her acceptance by email and looks forward to further news when the project is more advanced. Sarah replies with more details — the particular university which hosted the conference out of which all this arose, the likely publishing timetable, the terms regarding free offprints and the author discount on the final book. Naturally, Sarah sends the title as well; something with the right tone — abstract, pretentious and just a very slight, irresistible hint of what it's actually all about, *Truth and Transformation: Satire and Metamorphosis in the Early Eighteenth Century*. I reread this email now, more than six years after it was sent, and have the odd experience of almost believing it myself. Everything about it is right — it's a modest but perfect piece of the literary illusionist's art. It had to be good, for whatever else I've written, and whatever I write in the future this was the one occasion on which a certain talent for making things up truly mattered.

It's contact, but of the barest sort. Obsessively, I read over the two lines of Tomoko's reply, trying by some magical process to squeeze further information from it. I imagine a trail of data, bytes, electrons, the breadcrumbs of the digital world which must go back all the way to another keyboard which, when used to send this message, may have been no more than a few feet away from my children. Part of them has come with it, an infinitesimal, homeopathic dilution of their selves.

There are some practical problems with this deception: I have no interest in corresponding with Tomoko about the publication of an imaginary book, and she would certainly have no interest in corresponding with the real Douglas Galbraith. The lie must be maintained and at the same time developed to produce useful information. Sarah decides that the article must be re-typeset, and as this involves the possibility of errors creeping in, it will have to be proof-read again by Tomoko — could she have a postal address for sending the proofs? There's another lengthy, cagey silence before I get the next 'Dear Sarah . . .' And there it is, strangely easy — an enticing invitation to wade a little deeper into the lying game. For the first time in months I know where my children are: an apartment in a place called Toyonaka, just a few miles north of where they were before. It's a high-density suburb of Osaka, though not outstandingly grim or high-density by Japanese standards. With the help of the postcode I can pin them on a map to within a few tens of metres. I look it up and get pictures of the locality from the net. I've seen worse, but my heart sinks as I look at them and the crime feels freshly magnified, against Satomi and Makoto more than against myself. Why take them there, why take everything away from them and replace it with this?

What should I do with this information? Grandly, I feel this is like a piece of wartime Ultra intelligence — what matters most is that the enemy should never know I have it and should certainly never know how I got it. But this isn't a war, in spite of appearances, and all I care about is that my children should know as soon as possible that their father, mentally at least, is always with them. I send presents, revealing by doing so that I have found their new location. I send letters begging for photographs and receive a reply from Tomoko demanding money but regretting that her camera isn't working. I send a camera. Apparently, this one doesn't work either.

There doesn't seem to be anything more I can do. Weeks go by, perhaps a couple of months before I receive an unexpected message: 'Dear Sarah, How are you? It's a long time since I heard anything and I'm wondering how the book is coming on?' Only then do I realise that Tomoko has never connected my knowledge of her address with the fictional Sarah Levi and the much-desired book. Sarah Levi is still as real for Tomoko as I am to you, or you to me – she can still perform one last service.

It's a legal one, in a way. My 2004 consists of a public show of survival, an automatic persistence in writing novels. I finish in 1930s China and then let the robot arm swing over to pick up some new materials as I begin to assemble a new product. Alongside this performance another mindless machine joins in – the law itself, like those metallic bad guys you see in the movies, the ones that are always coming back to life when the protagonists are sure they've finally killed them. The dismissal of one set of lawyers brought a momentary satisfaction, but achieved nothing and I am compelled to hire the B-team to finish the job. The ghastly machine powers up again and lumbers on. The new lot seem to type their own letters rather than dictate them to Deirdre's provincial sister. Certainly, they are orthographically challenged and sentences occasionally tail off into next Thursday's proof and the points you raised in your. Before starting up again in perky professional cliché, oblivious to the fact that half the letter is meaningless. But they're more biddable, less arrogantly overpriced and good enough for what is, these days, a routine task.

The job in question is to find a way through the ethical

desert of one of the central elements of the new deal between men and women – no-fault divorce. There are good reasons for the wholesale change to this system over the last few decades. A modern, better educated and more assertive citizenry was no longer willing to accept burdensome state interference in their personal relations. Without this tactical retreat to divorce on demand, it is likely that the yoke of civil marriage would have been thrown off as briskly as that of ecclesiastical authority had been a couple of generations previously. The concession extended the life of relationship regulation, an extension now surely wearing thin as developed societies make their way to a post-marriage future. The change also put an end to the old-fashioned farce of staging one's own discovery in flagrante in order to provide the required evidence of adultery, and the unfairness of requiring a public admission of fault by one party in what was often divorce by mutual agreement.

There is a small constituency that yearns for a revival of old certainties, but it consists of people whose company one would not, on the whole, wish to share. Their agendas are more about social reaction than reform and are marked by an unattractive nostalgia for a more punitive past. They favour the newspapers that offer fixed-format tales of unwise and possibly confused ninety-seven-year-old Texan oil billionaires who marry eighteen-year-old 'former' prostitutes and crystal meth addicts only to divorce them six months later when they come upon them loudly rutting with their personal trainer while simultaneously arranging for their husband's assassination over a cellphone in the gaps between breathless yelps. Needless to say, the girl's lawyer explains that the phrase 'dead meat' referred only to a pizza order and that 'no fault' means 'no fault', which means half the money. There's enjoyable anger and head-shaking agreement that the world's gone mad. This never actually happens; not exactly. But while these caricatures are easy to dismiss we shouldn't take our eye off the fact that the move to no-fault systems has replaced one set of legal fictions with another, fictions which in some cases are very remote from underlying realities. An inflexible application of pragmatic and time-saving rules can seem like part of the rush to empty relationships of their moral content. Sharp injustices sometimes result and in the few cases that involve parental abductions these can stretch to the extreme ends of the spectrum.

'What?'

It's my new man on the phone, reporting on early skirmishes with the local judiciary.

'He thinks it's a desertion. It would mean waiting two years and then getting a divorce by default.'

'You've told him she abducted the children to Japan?'

'Oh, yes – all the papers are in.'

'And?'

'Well . . .'

It's one of those elongated 'wells' – the ones with plenty of give in the vowels, intended to signal that you should brace yourself for what's coming next.

'Well, he doesn't think it's relevant.'

And with that phrase I slip through the moral looking glass into the upturned world of modern matrimonial law.

The facts are not in dispute – why should they ever be in a fault-free world? Tomoko's submission to the court readily admits that she removed our children from the country by deception and without consent. She explains, with admirable candour, that she did this because (a) she felt like it, and (b) because of the poor quality of the sushi available from the local Tesco. Sadly for connoisseurs of the law's madnesses, this case would never come to judgment and so the diet-related defence of child abduction remains untested in Scotland. The argument, in any case, is not about these things and is not even directly about children – it is about money. In particular it is about the house, the house Tomoko also tried to sell in advance of her disappearance, along with the sofa, ushering various estate agents around the place as I plodded on in the study.

'But, my dear,' I would ask, still the hopeless innocent. 'Why sell it? Where would we go? What's the point of wasting these people's time?'

There would be a distracting rant on some other subject or an airy waving away of this frivolous objection.

And so the house, and the money it represents, remains in the jurisdiction and becomes a proxy for the whole issue. In divorce actions arising from international parental abductions, left-behind assets are a special case and should be recognised as such by the courts. They are often the only leverage on the abducting parent and should be available to negotiate better compromises on contact and communication with the abducted children – those whose interests the law claims to prioritise. For the intending abductor the thought of what might be a large material sacrifice could deter them. Conversely, where no-fault principles are applied with a strict amorality and even parental abduction is considered irrelevant, the intending abductor can go ahead without financial anxieties, confident that if they take the children first the courts will send the money on afterwards. This strong signal of indifference is interpreted by the abductor mentality as approval: it highlights that the exit door is always open and that there is no downside to bolting through it when relationships are under strain. Family lawyers can accurately inform their clients that it is a penalty free option and the borderline between this information and positive advice on the benefits of skipping the jurisdiction will, from time to time, inevitably be blurred.

The combination of parental abduction and no-fault divorce often drifts further into moral weirdness when detailed financial demands are made. Here the tactics of the abducting parent overlap with the business model of the criminal kidnapper for ransom. Having broken up the family by abduction they then make additional financial demands on the grounds that they have burdened themselves with the costs of raising the stolen children. The ransom kidnapper, that guy in the video messages in the balaclava, the one who sends your loved one's minor body parts as a token of his sincerity, makes an altogether more rational offer. If you give him the money you get the hostage back. The parental kidnapper defending in a no-fault divorce action demands the money *and* the hostages. Another key difference is that they often have the law on their side rather than on their tail. Acceding to these demands forces the bereft parent to finance the break-up of their own family and deprives them of the resources to pursue any legal action abroad. This was precisely the position of Tomoko's lawyers and there was never any indication in preliminary hearings that it was considered outlandish or legally unviable. In the end, it was largely what she achieved.

I want to talk to my children. I want to hear their voices and tell them their father loves them. I want to say that what they have been told about their new life may not be true and that they must try hard to think for themselves. I want to tell them to be happy and make them laugh. To do this I have a disputed asset, the last piece on my side of the board — that, and Sarah Levi.

Divorce actions involve a lot of lying about money. Both sides do it, deny they are doing it, and say it's only the other side that's doing it. A weary judiciary becomes generally sceptical. It makes sense because to break down these lies with serviceable evidence can be an expensive process — all the more so in international cases which depend to a greater extent on unverifiable written claims submitted from afar. Tomoko foresaw this and took the financial paperwork with her as well as the children. She's confident she can say anything she likes and pleads a poverty as shamelessly fictional as Sarah herself.

In circumstances such as these playing by the rules means losing, so it's time for Sarah to fire off some more good news about that long-delayed book. She announces that it's almost ready to go and one last thing is needed — a brief CV or author biography, a shop-window display of professional attainments, the more detailed and up to date the better. I don't really expect this to work — it seems too transparent and I still haven't fully understood how easy people are to deceive. I needn't have worried: the reply comes quickly and could have been written to order. Tomoko tells Sarah she is employed by two separate Japanese universities, which is odd because she's telling the court she isn't employed at all. A couple of days later I am sitting in my solicitor's office and watching a smile broaden across his face. He looks up and removes his glasses with a gesture daringly close to a flourish.

'Leave this with me.'

There's a telephone call the next morning just after breakfast.

'Interesting developments.'

'Yes?'

Tomoko's solicitor has just resigned. It can't be any sense of queasiness at representing a child abductor – she's known that from the start. And it can hardly be the fact that her client has been lying – she must also have known that from an early stage. It can only be the additional technical detail of this being proved by Tomoko's own words. Sarah sympathises with her professional embarrassment and sends a final communication, a condolence card before vanishing back into the nothingness from which I had created her.

This news took me briefly to a strange and intense psychological place. I had finally had an effect on my opponent, landed a meaningful blow. It was an illusion, but a powerful one, physically changing me – a sudden, violent high as if someone had stuck a syringe in my arm and thrust down hard on the plunger. Although nothing really had been achieved, nothing won, it made the world very different for a few hours, the permanent cloudy cast of powerlessness breaking and a new light shining through. It's just a memory now, a surviving fragment of dark knowledge as well as an

"On the Internet, nobody knows you're a dog."

untrustworthy, dreamlike sense of what it might be to live like that all the time.

Another lawyer picks up the lucrative baton on Tomoko's behalf. This could go on indefinitely; a combination of the cab-rank rule and the perjury-free world of modern divorce proceedings means the dishonest litigant can switch from one legal taxi to another before continuing their journey with only the mildest inconvenience. It's the meter, ticking ever upwards, that dictates the final terms. But it's not quite true that nothing has changed – Sarah's last throw of the dice has certainly applied some pressure. The new lawyer must have explained to Tomoko that her fumble with the truth could weigh against her, that she might forfeit a little of the court's deep reserves of trust. Might it not be a good idea to manufacture some more positive evidence, proof of reasonableness, compromise? He must have had a struggle with this point – it is not the language of the parental abductor. But Tomoko does understand tactics, manipulation, the useful smile. Within a week or two, sitting down at the computer to resume the dreary wrestling match that is the current novel, I find a new message. I can see that it's from Japan and hesitate. I open it and find the telephone number I didn't dare to hope for.

This call makes a matched pair with the first one to the police. Nearly a year has passed and there I am again pacing in the kitchen, this time with the long international number in my hand. There is an appointed hour and I know it has come when I hear the pips on the radio. I turn down the volume and key in the twelve digits. There are clicks, a gap and then a foreign ring tone. Tomoko answers in Japanese, pretending that it might not be me. There's a frigid control in her voice – for anyone else this would be a costly performance, but for her there is no strain at all. It's Magda on the line, the eternal possessor of children. She launches at once into a lengthy complaint about the non-existence of Sarah Levi and all the trouble she has caused her. Her victimhood has remained pristine, conscienceless, completely untouched by anything she has done, as it always will be. I'm not interested in this and try to get past it, straining to pick up every tiny sound from the background as if, bat-like, the echoes will allow me to see. What is the room like, who else is in it? The television is playing quietly, a children's programme. Who is watching it, turning away from the screen as they notice their mother speaking English on the telephone? Tomoko tells me to wait. There are sounds of movement, the receiver being picked up, a small, silent, uncertain presence.

'Papa?'

The calls establish themselves on a fortnightly basis, mostly regular, sometimes disrupted according to whim or gamesmanship. They are part of an obscene bargain which trades control of assets for the right of two children to hear their father's voice. They are a means of another sort of control also, an invisible, long-distance puppeteer's thread stretching all the way from Japan to Scotland — which might explain why they went on as long as they did.

After further absurd delays the court procedure approaches its first climax, the possibility after eighteen months of bureaucratic, pompous and self-regarding preamble of a decision actually being made. With only a few days to go before this hearing an offer comes in, a modest concession with regard to the division of the house. I am warned of the difficulties in pushing the judiciary off their preferred rubber-stamp, fifty–fifty settlements, of my dangerous naivety in persisting with ethical beliefs in a no-fault world. When I suggest pushing the issue, campaigning through the appeal courts for the view that parental abduction should not be seen as morally neutral, I am coldly informed that I can't afford it. I am being manoeuvred into accepting this concession. Exhausted and distrustful of all my options, I take it.

The structure of our game is simplified. The house must still be sold, large sums of money still transferred to Japan, and alongside it all the fortnightly telephone call, the king on my board. Naturally, I will lose this too, but the agreement lacks a timetable – it can be a long game. I squat on the asset, refusing to let it be advertised for sale and every few months fending off a monstrously covetous estate agent in hot pursuit of commission. This lasts for a surprising length of time – more than two years, maybe nearer to three. But it can't be put off for ever and eventually the sale is made. Tomoko now has the children and the money and before long the telephone, predictably, goes dead. It has been an expensive exercise. Together, these telephone calls came to six figures, possibly the most expensive there have ever been. They were worth it.

*

This is everything to me, nothing to you – and if it were someone else's story I would be the one to stifle a yawn and make my apologies. It is part of what modernity means, part of what the new painters were on about when they said that only an image of jumbled, conflicting perspectives could convey the truth about the world. That old style looking-like-it-really-is stuff, with everyone agreeing on a single point of view, that was finished for ever. And so we now lead lives more deeply divided from each other than ever before – the parent from the childless, those anchored in families from those adrift, and at the most fundamental level of all, even the female from the male. At times they seem like separate stories, but this must be a mistake – it looks a mess, some say it is, but it's all happening within the same single context, within the same frame.

You and I perhaps once stood on the same station platform. It's not very likely but it's possible and if it wasn't you it would have been someone rather like you, living roughly in the same socio-economic space and more or less at the same time in history, subject to the same forces, the same images. There I am lagging behind you, an unnoticeable person vaguely thinking of writing the book you will read a few years later. I see what you see, by and large, and am looking over my shoulder so intently that I nearly trip on entering the train. Seated, I continue to peer out at the empty platform. Perhaps you follow my gaze, curious, keen not to miss out on a minor spectacle — but there's nothing there. Your fellow traveller's expression of astonishment remains a mystery.

It was an advertisement that suddenly seized my attention, the very same one you have seen and ignored many times. Until then I had ignored it too — the oddness, the essential inexplicability of the poster proclaiming the excellent deals to be had on family railcards always passing me by. It's how the dominant prejudices of the age work: they maintain their hold over our minds not by standing up to scrutiny, but by discouraging the fatal questions from being asked in the first place, sometimes for generations. The tactic resembles that of camouflage in nature. The prejudicial idea has no defence against reason except to elude the danger by being nearly identical to the background pattern of thought. It becomes part of the manners of the age — it is polite to express agreement with it; socially clumsy or even abrasive to question it. After such discourtesies one is not invited back. Vulnerable when exposed, it flourishes so long as it remains hidden – a blot on blot-patterned wallpaper, the old slyboots invisibly getting on with its dirty work until one day you catch sight of it out of the corner of your eye, out of a train window perhaps, creeping up on you, finally giving itself away.

There are two messages, at least, in many images – the open and the less open – and either can be the more powerful. On the surface of this one I see that the purchasers of the Family Railcard have obviously been enjoying their day out. As the product is beneficial to all ages I see two generations of women standing behind and protectively embracing two children – a girl and her younger brother. Everyone is smiling – an image of complete, railway-assisted satisfaction. It's family life at its best. But as the train moves off and the other and more important message seeps in, I ask myself just when it was that we drifted into a society in which it became normal to portray the family as fatherless? As we skirt East Lomond and head south I become more and more fixated on the lower part of the poster, on the children and their unpromising futures. There she is – grown to maturity as the typical custodial parent, always tired, always worried about money. And there he is, or isn't – a grown man cut out of his own family photographs by forces that have been at work since his own childhood.

Once attuned to these messages I detect them more frequently. A mortgage is advertised on the grounds of its particular convenience. A woman in her early forties and her ten-year-old son are leaning on the edge of a swimming pool and smiling into the camera lens. Clearly, everything is rosy in this life and the strapline confirms it: 'I'm happy mine's sorted'. What does it mean? It must refer, most obviously, to her finances, perhaps to her holiday plans with her son. But it has a wider meaning too – her life is 'sorted', simplified after the divorce that has left this more manageable sub-nuclear family. This is confirmed by the company's other slogan, 'built around you', the personal pronoun here unmistakcably singular. The image addresses itself to the winners and to their thoroughly modern, self-fulfilled happiness. This is, to a degree, what is being sold as well as the mortgage.

The male does not have to be absent, to get the idea across. He still remains a favoured character in the marketing of life insurance. The problem here is that he's been given the black spot even before things have started. He appears as classic provider, but only in a pre-death sort of way, marking the future absence which will be made good by the proceeds of the policy you are invited to buy. Another, and equally valid, view of this approach is to see it as anti-feminist, especially those versions equipped with a simpering Stepford wife whose only source of income is to marry it or dance the merry widow on its grave, cheque in hand. Neither interpretation does much for the durability of modern relationships.

In other areas the male has made an impressive comeback in the microdramas of the advertising world, and nowhere more so than in telecommunications. Whereas once the telephone was sold in the context of female loquacity, it has now shifted to male absence: the male has become the essential phone user because it's the only way he can talk to his children. One storyline finds humour in an absent father unexpectedly learning from his young daughter that she is going to a wedding – her mother's wedding to a new partner. The revelation of a new male being invited into his child's living space, essentially the revelation of his own final replacement as a parent, is presented as an amusing embarrassment for the mother and as a piece of charming naivety on the part of the child. In real life this situation would have at its heart a great deal of failure, pain and deception. That it should appear in an advertisement, in an inducement to buy the goods or services of the sponsor, suggests that the normalisation of the new distance between men and women has gone a long way indeed.

Images are powerful in sneakily nudging us towards convictions, but language is more powerful still, and in all the language of the emotions there is surely nothing more loaded than the language of mothering. Mothered, mother-love, loved him like a mother and, for the less fortunate in life, only a mother could love him. Motherland is good, fatherland always has boots on and a helmet and a disagreeable marching style. And this planet is not the only offender – we know that in a galaxy far, far away the X-Wing Fighters are always returning to the mother ship. What is mother-love, what does it mean? Is it bigger than the other sentimental bonds, a different size or colour? Does it have a different atomic number, or its ions a different valency, can we spot it on the microscope slide, a blue Gram-positive dot of loveliness standing out amongst the inferior species? The language is so constant and pervasive that it must mean something, surely – think how offended people would be if it turned out to be no more than a theology of the emotions, endless talk of nothing.

Perhaps this is too literal-minded an approach. It may be that mother-love is not really a thing at all, not a mass or force in the natural world but a claim, the assertion of a privilege in the way that property is never the thing in itself but the proprietor's claim to it. This certainly fits the usage of mothering language more accurately, and it might still be reasonable if we could detect something especially valuable and unique about the female parent rather than the male, an objective natural fact that would give the mother a right to barge to the front of the queue whenever the refinement and preciousness of emotional lives is at issue. We readily accept comparable claims elsewhere, allowing that the more thirsty should go first when there is a drought and that the lean should precede the fat when there is a famine. We accept also that for any particular role the more competent can fairly be preferred, however many other issues intrude in practice.

The problem is that mothering language goes far beyond this to make a general claim to parental superiority thereby disparaging both the caring capacities of fathers and the intensity of their emotional lives with regard to their children. If these claims are true there will be evidence that they are true and a careful study will detect that evidence, or its absence. The difficulty is that it is hard to see just how such an experiment could be designed. Evidence could not be gathered by asking people any more than the truth of a religion could be assessed by questioning its devotees. Even a more remote study of gender and parenting in developed societies would see only the social norms in action, including the effect of biased language heard from infancy by all the experimental subjects. The search for clean data might ultimately lead us to abandon humanity altogether and search for answers in the culturally uncontaminated family lives of mountain gorillas and chimpanzees. My own detailed knowledge extends only to a data set of one – my own life. Here I can find no evidence of anything dilute or second-rate or expendable in my relationship with my children, or in their relationship with me. On the contrary, it was the strength of those bonds that motivated their mother to break them.

Amongst legislators the mothering virus also continues its work, often surprisingly immune to the prevailing norms of non-discrimination. An obscure but typical instance can be found in a British Parliamentary Working Party report from the early 1990s examining the problem of parental abduction. The suggestions for dealing with it include – 'Threatened parents should tell teachers, other mothers and school friends that their child must not be collected by anyone other than themselves . . .' The implication of 'other mothers' appears to be invisible to the authors, suggesting that only female parents can be trusted to collect their children from school and that all threats in such situations are male – an idea flatly contradicted by the facts of modern parental abduction. The effect of such advice is to facilitate parental abductions by negligently ushering through the female abductor. I should have been the one to warn against people collecting my children from school.

Mothering language retains its prevalence long after the child has grown up. A few months ago, while making notes for this chapter I wondered if I was slipping into a psychotic episode as the television started to make editorial suggestions from the corner of the room. I turned to see what was going on and found a news item from Wootton Bassett, the small English town that has recently become known for its public displays of respect for the remains of dead British soldiers brought back from Afghanistan to the nearby RAF base at Lyneham. A journalist did a short piece to camera before comments from bystanders were edited in. They were asked to explain why they were there, why it was important to them. As another cortège passed in the background a woman explained she was there 'for all those mums of these soldiers . . .' As it was not a live piece, someone must have reviewed and approved this for broadcast. They must have chosen it, knowing full well that it would be heard by the bereaved fathers of the same young soldiers.

Like other deeply rooted languages of prejudice this hurts people, facilitates injustice and is often wrong in fact. The language of mothering is love's casual sexism. We should try harder to recognise it for what it is and do more to change it. The process has begun, but is still at its earliest stages – a mild increase in awareness, a slight raising of one eyebrow as a listener hears the routine unfairness of it all but doesn't yet feel able to question it. In the longer term the gendered sanctity of motherhood cannot sustain itself as a plausible idea. Exclusively female control of child-rearing will result in exclusively female responsibility for the consequences: women will find themselves blamed for negative outcomes, if only because so many men will have an alibi.

6 *In the grown-up world*

Existence is new and empty; you are its god. From somewhere — let's not cavil over the details — you receive an instruction to create the ultimate in vulnerability, a machine for getting hurt which can never be bettered. You settle down to think about it for an age or two — there is no template or model for such a creature; you are free in your omnipotence to perfect it as you please. What qualities must the finished article have? It must have a great capacity for pain and an even greater one for fear. It must bruise easily and carry the internal mark of such injuries long after they have superficially healed. It must be too trusting so that it is easy to lie to and mislead. It must be unduly forgiving so that it can be abused again and again without the lessons of suspicion or calculation ever being learned. It must be hopeful beyond all reason so that the pain of repeated disappointment is never lessened. It must have many basic needs, of which it can easily be deprived. It must be weak and little regarded by others so that it can neither defend itself nor obtain allies to act on its behalf. Above all — and what a genius refinement this is — it must offer to the world an unlimited and indiscriminate love so that it is drawn to whatever is nearby and resembles it, even when that object of attraction is its own tormentor. As the architect of such a creature you might make it any size or colour or shape imaginable — these are matters of mere whim. But what is certain is that the inner life of this piece of work would be something we would recognise immediately as being very like that of a human child. How should such a creature be treated?

There should be good answers to this question; after all, it is more agonised over now than ever before. There is also a greater diversity of answers – the ancient and unchanged alongside the newest problems of freedom and surplus, neolithic childhoods in some parts of the world contemporary with debates elsewhere about computer games and social networking sites. Which is best, and what can one learn from the other, if anything? Are the trends positive, or are we just finding new and more luxurious paths to failure? There is no consensus. A rhetorician could gather support for a 'common-sense' approach, though there would be no agreement as to what common sense is. The field attracts the guru and the pundit. Science is applied, but may struggle not to be crowded out by pseudo-science. Agendas abound, solutions are peddled, sheep fleeced. The media recount the extremes as if they represent a general malaise. At times one would think that the whole cacophony expresses only our anxiety rather than the attempt to find a way forward in good faith.

Where does the child stand now as a member of one of the weakest minorities in the adult world, what is the direction of travel? There are two ways of measuring this, each valid, even when contradictory. One is to look at the public space – laws, conventions, the distribution of resources and of power. The other is memory, the inner record of what it was like to be a child in the past and the comparison of that with today's scene – where is the progress and where, correcting as best we can for nostalgia, the regress?

I approach forty-five years of age as I write this – already more than old enough to recall changes in something that, for much of human history, has remained relatively stable. For me, my childhood is what I am conscious of as childhood and that means it starts with earliest memories – I would suppose about 1968 or 1969 – and ends with puberty and the widening out of awareness to the rest of the world. The end of my childhood had something to do with the wave of strikes in Britain known as the Winter of Discontent in 1979. Being driven by my father past vast mounds of uncollected rubbish through a permanently dark Glasgow towards a private school in the city's west end had something to do with the end of my childhood. Becoming aware that the custard-yellow Mercedes Benz in which I was travelling was now socially as well as literally conspicuous was also a part of that end. It had something to do with the election of Margaret Thatcher and the Islamic Revolution in Iran and then the humiliation of Carter in the United States and his replacement by Ronald Reagan – an awareness that things could fail, slip backwards, even for a whole national generation as a result of a brief, callous exercise of power or democratic misjudgement. It had something to do with the Boomtown Rats singing 'I Don't Like Mondays'; something to do with sleeping sweetly through the Vietnam War and waking up to all this.

That makes my childhood about eleven years long. I can't say that it was packed with incident and excitement, but feel that its large blanks must have been reasonably happy – neither storing up gold for the tests of adult life, nor laying down too many of the scars and inhibitions that hold people back. Being educated in Scotland and in the private sector I caught the last, vicious flick of the tail from the Dickensian ethic. My experience of primary education was mostly one of fear and sudden, arbitrary violence handed out by adults to small children. We existed resiliently in a world where, because we were children, it was neither reasonable nor possible to prevent adults from hurting us whenever, in adult judgement, it was necessary. The monopoliser of legitimate violence – our first lesson in the concept of the state – was the headmistress, an aquiline, embittered woman with frighteningly dyed blue-black hair and a vigorously athletic approach to punishment. She would batch-beat seven- and eight-year-olds with a rigid, quarter-inch-thick leather strap, lining them up in her office four or five at a time. As this room had a fully glazed French window that opened on to the playground there would always be an eager crowd of onlookers pressing up against the glass and giving the drama a public element – an element that in her mind, no doubt, added to its utility. She went at it with a will, face tight with the strain as she began her full, golf-swing movement, finally making contact with a sharp and, if she got it just right, shockingly loud detonation. By the time she had worked her way to the end of the line she was breathless, perspiring, slightly trembling, eyes bright, stimulated in a way we were in no position to understand or, for that matter, care about.

The headmistress employed her sister in the same establishment: a woman whose professional life therefore involved daily subjugation to her sibling. Her inferior status was symbolised by the fact that she had no authority to belt the children. She made do with a knuckleduster instead, cunningly disguised as costume jewellery. Her right fist was equipped with a number of rings set with large, cheap stones – amethysts, cairngorms and the like, the larger the better. With these she would punch the offender in the side of the head, accompanying the assault with a metrical stream of abuse on the theme of his total worthlessness as a human being. I don't suppose she used a great deal of force, but we got the message all the same: that the right to defend oneself was for grown-ups and all we could do was endure and wait until we joined their ranks and began, ourselves, to enjoy their privileges.

Something over thirty years later the telephone rings. It's her again, the eternal headmistress, though there has been a small adjustment in our language in the meantime and she is now a head teacher. Her tone is grave and I understand that it is her sad duty to convey some enormity to me. I prepare myself. Satomi has been giving concern.

'Yes?'

Is it the paraquat in the tea-urn prank? Has he wired the minibus to explode at anything less than 70 miles per hour? He's a very bright boy and I've been encouraging his scientific curiosity – only the other day I showed him how to set things on fire with a magnifying glass. Perhaps it's all my fault. Is the school in ashes?

It turns out that Satomi, in all his six-year-old self-confidence, has had a difference of opinion with the head teacher. He has decided to stand his ground, fold his arms across his chest, stare the woman down and say 'No!' in a tone that reverberates through the school as a revolutionary act. Because this is witnessed by other children it risks an

outbreak of general disorder. As I listen with all due solemnity, my mind drifts to a vision of the primary school version
of *If* . . . — Satomi hosing down the place with automatic fire
while pulling the pin from a grenade with his teeth before
lobbing it in the direction of the fleeing staff. That's my boy.

'Of course. I quite understand. No, indeed — we can't have
that at all.'

I agree to deliver a lecture on the virtues of co-operation.
Satomi takes this stoically, maintaining his integrity by
saying nothing at all as I perjure myself, trying all the time
to conceal how pleased I am by his powers of resistance.
How vividly I remember being in his position — on so many
occasions — loomed over by one of these outsized foreigners.
What did they mean, what did they want? Could you trust
them, whose side were they on? Why couldn't they just
leave us alone? I add some refresher comments the next
morning before wrapping him up in my arms and sending
him on his way with a kiss. I watch him run for the little
bus which can practically fit the whole school in its dozen
or eighteen seats; he has a chrome yellow top and a blue
backpack, a darting patch of sun and sky. I hear no more —
the problem is solved.

These vignettes, repeatable many thousands of times
over, record a significant change between the adult and child
generations — one well worth remembering when listening
to gloomy assessments of contemporary childhood. It is
partly a matter of culture that has brought about these
changes, but also more formal campaigns to extend human
rights to the child — specifically the right to equal treatment
under the law generally and with regard to assault in

particular. It was the law rather than custom that banned corporal punishment from state schools in the United Kingdom from 1987 onwards. Wealthier parents could continue to have their children beaten in private schools for a few years longer, but even that was eventually banned. The issue stands for a wider trend: a slow and often reluctant drift away from the child's special legal status, special in being selected for a lower level of protection in an adult world run according to adult rules.

Away from school, life was always happier, freer – but it is here that the changes over the last few decades make a stronger case for concern about contemporary childhood. I lived in a one-screen household, the screen in question being a Bush colour television stolidly encased in a teak-effect cabinet. It had four buttons, three of which showed programmes while the fourth, mysteriously labelled ITV2, never did. This button referred obscurely to the future, though no one quite understood how. Watching it was a communal affair and often a very dull one at that. Perhaps we looked forward to making more individual and diverse choices without ever doubting that to be bored separately might turn out to be so much worse than being bored together; essentially the same experience as before, but without the compensation of having fellow sufferers by your side. The enforced narrowness gave people common ground. That doesn't go very far in justifying it, but we now know it wasn't worthless either.

To walk away from this focal point was to walk away from the fire and light your own somewhere else – a highly signifi-cant move that always left both parties, the dissident and the abandoned majority, gamely pressing on through *The Black and White Minstrel Show*, with a sense of rejection. I walked away to books — a decision that was part of my childhood and then, as the books grew up, part of its end also. This moment in family life is rare now because the focal point itself has gone. It started to weaken with the introduction of multiple televisions into the household, most perniciously into the child's bedroom — always an act of neglect on the part of the parent, never one of provision or care. Today, a scene of the family at rest in the wireless broadband household, with the hand-me-down laptops taken over by the children, typically has people pointing in different directions, oriented away from each other and towards their own private screens. Much of this is good and useful — certainly, it is powerfully attractive. I feel the addict's weakness of will ebbing away even in the middle of this sentence as I break off to check my email, or how my guano futures are doing, or the amazing fact that some dross I'm unloading on eBay still hasn't received any bids. We want it, of course, and always more. But sometimes we want it too much and then it becomes the obesity of distraction.

For the child the multi-screen world offers new and earlier opportunities to separate himself from family and the adult world, tuning out of all common interests, tuning in only to his own — interests which are often no more than the dictates of fashion, marketing spend, or the latest 'viral' novelty. It's better than being bored watching someone else's favourite programmes, but as an experience it's a miserable substitute for reality. Today, from the earliest age, we are encouraged to confuse the nature of screens and windows, forgetting that until very recently a screen always hid the world from view. It is more ambiguous now, but it hasn't wholly lost that earlier function. Arguably, it is regaining it in new ways.

Even the single screen wasn't up to much as far as I was concerned, and I enjoyed all my most intense experiences as a child outside the home, where I exercised a freedom that seems to have been in steady decline for the last thirty years. It was brief – perhaps just three summers at its height, my Huckleberry Finn days. The paedophile had not yet been invented as a media phenomenon – presumably the real ones were there, but the imaginary ones hadn't yet started their work and the whole smothering hypochondria of childhood safety was still in the future. My friends and I had the range and lifestyle of feral cats, wandering over our territory from park to disused quarry, to building sites and railway lines and the council transport depot, the one with a telegraph pole in the corner with a large grey and red rotary siren on the top to tell you when the nuclear bombs were coming. We lived close to the ground, always finding small things of interest by our feet and returning muddy and leaf-littered from where we had crouched in some depression, watching the grown-ups go by on the path no more than a yard or two from where we spied on them, as silent and invisible as wild animals. I read science fiction that explained how two civilisations could live in different dimensions, cheek by jowl, alien to each other and unsuspecting of each other's existence until some disruption tore open the membranes that kept them apart and catastrophe ensued. I wasn't sure it was just a theory.

Fire was my thing – I loved it, and never feared it. My

mind was full of fantasy novels in which heroes and villains exercised their will directly on the world by magic and in the half-reality, half-dream of childhood fire was magic and transformation, its control was power. It also met one other essential requirement: it was an axiom of my childhood that whatever was worth doing was something an adult wanted you not to do. The sportsman in us relished this opposition, and the opposition of the whole responsible, killjoy, adult world was as good as it got. We knew the adult world was firmly against the child fire-stealer.

As a ten-year-old it would have embarrassed me to leave the house without a box of matches and a blade. Today I am often baffled by the current generation of censors when they deplore the dangers of video games – games whose most unsatisfactory characteristic is surely their total lack of danger, unless one considers addictive, mesmeric tedium to be a danger in itself. I might be more interested if anything ever really burst into flames as a result of playing a video game, but I don't believe it does. This extremism no doubt derives from my child self who would have been unimpressed by the inauthenticity of the screen experience precisely because he knew what it was to throw a real Molotov cocktail. The skills of mid-seventies boyhood – as I remember them – certainly included borrowing plastic tubing from the ubiquitous home-brew kit, siphoning petrol from a couple of vehicles, taxing the local addresses two or three bottles each from the back step and repairing to a nearby railway bridge to launch our incendiary attack against the wall at the other side. We knew the fluttering noise of the burning wick as the bottle arced through the air and the blast of heat and light as it smashed and exploded, the existential moment of recoiling from your own destructive achievement.

I was ambitious to go further and grasped from an early age that knowledge was power and that some fields were more powerful than others. While schoolwork was an imposition, a yoke laid across the shoulders of an economic unit, I sensed that there was a secret opposite to this, rebellion's white magic that would fend off the adult world's empire of dullness. I rapidly mastered the *Encyclopaedia Brittanica*'s helpful article on explosives and set about putting the information to good use. In those days it was a simple matter to spin a tale in a hardware shop and come out with twenty pounds of a white crystalline powder that is no longer obtainable in pure form – and for very good reasons. With the help of this enchanting substance, and some basic metalworking skills, my collaborators and I manufactured numerous small pipe bombs, the deployment of which delighted us almost as much as real powers of sorcery might have done. To be near one of these when they went off was quite an experience. They were no mere fireworks, creating a punchy blast wave and a ringing in the ears for half a minute or more afterwards. Occasionally there was the bonus of a low hum overhead as a shred of red-hot copper or stainless steel whizzed by as we hit the deck. In most childhoods this is no more than a sound effect on a TV show or in the cinema. Not for us – we had the real thing. No doubt a primatologist would recognise in this a form of auditory scent-marking – a declaration of territory that could be heard for miles in every direction, the sort of thing a howler

monkey would do if you gave it a chemistry set and some
easy-to-follow instructions.

The membrane separating the child and adult dimensions did tear one day, the two alien species coming across
one another in dramatic astonishment. We had just brought
off a pleasingly large explosion in the wooded edge of a golf
course and were pelting out of cover when we ran straight
into a foursome of golfers. These blasts were impressive
enough if you knew what was coming, but to be suddenly
struck by one without warning was genuinely shocking. I
remember a golf ball still balanced on a yellow plastic tee,
and a club on the ground beside it where the player had
dropped it in fright. This man looked more affected than the
others and was so white he must have been close to fainting.
Several disoriented seconds passed before the golfers decided
the explosion and the small boys in front of them must be
connected. It was the man whose shot had been so uniquely
disturbed, the man who had been most humiliated by our
intervention, who picked up his club and came at me,
shoving me to the ground with enough force to send me
rolling over several times. The other golfers approached, one
of them shouting to his colleague, frightened that he was
about to lose control, to go too far. And so I looked up from
where I lay on the grass at this lumbering, breathless,
club-wielding creature and enjoyed a moment of pure,
autonomous childhood. My heart was racing, but I can't
remember any fear that the encounter was going to go badly
for our side. I was equipped in the usual way for those days — a
knife in one pocket and two or three small explosive devices
in another. While in reality they would have done nothing

for me against an adult with a golf club, reality wasn't where I lived. I had confidence in them as a primitive or a believer would have confidence in a charm. Besides, we were whippet quick and knew the ground thereabouts much better than these portly car salesmen and bidet merchants – we could still fit through all the gaps long since barred to them. I got to my feet and began to walk backwards slowly, in the manner advised for dealing with aggressive dogs. When my friends and I had achieved a sufficient distance, we issued empty threats about reporting them to the police for assault, added some vibrantly obscene abuse for good measure and then vanished back into the undergrowth just as the dense white smoke from the explosion oozed from the trees and drifted sluggishly across the course.

What did they make of us, I wonder, irrupting into their world with this deafening stage effect, unmotivated, inexplicable and downright dangerous before disappearing again with only the smoke as certain evidence that it had ever really happened? Something halfway to the supernatural, I shouldn't wonder – one of those minor species of the other world that every culture invents as the invisible explanation for why things go wrong, why the seemingly inanimate resists us. Also, something disturbing about still being free, about not having settled for the only crummy deal on offer, about not yet having failed.

One would not recommend such entertainments for the contemporary child, if only out of reluctance to take responsibility for the inevitable casualties. Besides, the world has somewhat lost its sense of humour on the subject of explosives in the last few years – one regrettable, if relatively minor consequence of which has been the discouragement of scientific curiosity in a new generation of children. When such adventures go wrong it's a news story, but A Hundred Million Children all Across the Industrialised World Get Bored and Fat Sitting at Home in Front of a Screen is a news story too, or should be. Certainly, it involves harm, psychological as well as physical. Meanwhile, we continue to marshal our children away from improbable or non-existent dangers towards the half-hearted joys of the organised activity and the washed-out world of the virtual rather than the real.

When my boys were taken I fear they not only lost their home and their father, but also moved forward in time into this less free, ersatz childhood. The height of Satomi's mischief was water-pistolling some nearby cows with a friend – the animals were mildly refreshed. The miscreants jumped as I arrived on the scene, unsure what to expect. We chatted for a while and I left them to get on with it. What I fear is that my older son will remember so trivial an event as a marker, not of happier times, but of what was prematurely lost and can't now ever be restored. Both he and his brother would have gone on to greater crimes and rebellions. As their father I would have tried to keep them safe, but not to the extent of being less than fully alive. Now I can only assume that they are in the screened world, shuttling between apartment and school, the working single parent present at evenings and weekends only, the sumo television dominating the tiny Japanese living room. It's all very twenty-first century, though it could have been different. These things have happened, after all, not as a result of a force of nature but of bad choices, as a result of accepting what we were once free to reject.

Poring over a map of where I believe they are living I can see what I would have seen as a child – a chance for revolt. I hope they take it, while they still have the spirit. I imagine the two brothers bunking off on a school day, laden with stashed food, a knife and the means to make fire as they take the other train, the one that goes north past Kawanishi and on to the end of the line at Nissei-chuo. At that time in the morning they are the only people travelling away from the city. They've had no reason to go that way before and within a couple of stops they're in another country where all the decisions will be theirs. They shin over the fence at the end of the station car park and follow any upward incline. They cross the creeping mange of golf courses that eats away at what remains of Japan's natural world, moving from cover to cover to avoid the early players, feeling instincts they didn't know they had drop neatly into place. They move from fairway to rough, across the out of bounds line, up into the trees. It starts as industrial plantation, but as they work their way up hour by hour it turns at last into a real forest.

They choose a patch of ground which they know is good from the toppled stones of an old Shinto shrine not on any map. Here they stage their rebellion, subsisting on Meiji chocolate bars and tofu, smokily toasted on sticks over their own fire. They wake to find themselves being observed by a family of wild boar and one evening run like never before from what they thought might be a bear, though they never had time to turn and see for sure. But it was, really, as Makoto tells it later: he could feel the featherlight stroke of its claws between his shoulder blades, a millimetre short of leaving a permanent mark. They escape with their lives, like something they have discovered for the first time. After three days the chocolate has run out and it's not so much fun any more. They wander down the mountain and get the train back into town. And there they stand, filthy, exhausted, with new knowledge, allied in their contempt for the lecture about how much trouble they have caused, which washes over them as they reject the demands for an apology and don't even try to look as if they give a damn. That's what I want for them — the substance of a future anecdote. But I don't suppose it will happen now, not these days.

In my own childhood it is the non-memories that indicate the greatest change — no memory of a sense of insecurity, no memory of the fear that my life would be turned upside down by decisions made by adults on an adult agenda, the sort of decisions presented as 'best for all concerned' despite plainly being a selfish and dishonest failure. An illness might have thrown my life into turmoil, a traffic accident, or even a bankruptcy but not a deliberate, avoidable choice that would suddenly have snatched me from the familiar to the strange. There was never any risk of that, never even an unfounded fear that it might happen, and not because my parents' marriage was always easy, but because they knew it wasn't only for themselves. My first encounter with the social revolution of individualism — a revolution already well under way — was later, though still in my school years. Of the millions of words exchanged between me and my young colleagues only a handful have remained as memories. I would guess that they mostly belong to Mondays — the first opportunity to speak after the weekend's revelations from the older generation. One was 'I'm adopted', and another was

'My parents are getting divorced'. My response was gauche, unhelpful; it was the first time I had heard such a thing. Now it is not uncommon for the parent–teacher meeting to be rendered awkward by the fact that two of the people there – in the unlikely event that they have both turned up – can hardly bear to be in the same room.

And so memory delivers a mixed report: childhood in the modern world isn't going to the dogs, it just isn't going anywhere very much. This is not a good result – stasis over the ensuing thirty years is not what people looked forward to when my childhood was ending in the late 1970s. This is at the heart of our doubts – that through a lengthy period of peace and economic expansion the most essential non-material goods of life have either drifted or been allowed to deteriorate as they have been de prioritised in favour of economic goals. It appears to be what we wanted. As the lines of GDP per capita and family breakdown ascend together across the post-war graph, it might be that the most obvious explanation is the right one – that our age is defined by the conscious choice of money over love.

Some non-materialistic causes have found a voice; others have retained one from older, though now weakened traditions. What is left of churches in the developed world allows for a source of social commentary and questioning by a body of men and women who do at least have non-financial measures of success and failure, however outmoded the basis of their ideas. In looking for a new and rational set of non-financial values only the green movement presents itself as a plausible candidate. Anti-globalisation has remained too unfocused, inarticulate and recreational in its protests to be effective. It's hard then, to get the ball rolling in public affairs without the money link and that must explain why one of those other non-material causes we would expect people to take seriously, that of the rights and well-being of children, has continued to be muted and lacking in fresh ideas. An awareness of this called for a grand gesture and it took the form of the United Nations Convention on the Rights of the Child – the first document of its kind and one which entered history at the remarkably late date of 1989.

The Convention is billed as legally binding but is, more realistically, an exhortation to do good things and to suffer no consequences if you don't. It's valuable as a benchmark and an encouragement to the well-meaning, but wholly untroubling to the authoritarian or the moral foot-dragger who despises its values even as he signs up. It is cleverly drafted as a sort of legal algorithm – you can insert any variables into it you please, but it always produces the same output of zero as far as enforceable results go. The document tacks through a series of prevarications and self-contradictions before finally committing suicide in Article 41, which asserts the superiority of national laws in any case, thus completely evacuating it of any real content. The diplomat smiles pityingly at these objections and explains, reasonably enough, that if it weren't empty no one would have signed it. The Convention does have the distinction of being the most widely accepted human rights agreement, with only two governments remaining outside the fold: the government of Somalia, which barely exists, and the government of the United States, which until very recently remained desirous of executing juveniles.

The Convention is a promise from the powerful to the weak and as such it sometimes has that expansive, open-handed quality familiar from colonial treaties between white men with guns and indigenous peoples without guns — it's not that the negotiators didn't mean it at the time, it's just that they knew they wouldn't have to go through with it later if it turned out to be inconvenient. In other words, it's an adult's promise to a child and is therefore inherently unreliable. Early on, it declares the best interests of the child to be a primary consideration — fashionable language at the time, with a similar phrase appearing at the head of the United Kingdom's Children Act of the same year. Rhetorically, it's a hands-down winner, always enthusiastically endorsed by anyone intent on elbowing their way to the head of a manipulable mob and seizing control of their agenda with the demand 'Won't somebody please think of the children?' Who could reject such an appeal? No one, it seems, apart from Somalia and the United States.

There are worthy clauses about banning 'all forms of physical violence' against children, but it is illustrative of the text's fear of precision that corporal punishment is not specifically mentioned, leaving it unclear as to whether the ghost of my old headmistress is now an international as well as a domestic law-breaker. My scepticism rises when I note articles about the right of children to be heard in legal proceedings — is that heard and ignored, or heard and respected? The latter would imply a potential prohibition on divorce where there are dependent children and those children clearly express the view that such a move would be against their interests, as many of them might. But there is no prospect of such a real concession of legal power from the adult to the child. The idea may be described as a right but it is, in reality, no more than a condescension. Elsewhere, I note declarations that children should not be separated from their parents against their will and that, if they are separated from one or both, the signatories will respect the child's right 'to maintain personal relations and direct contact with both parents on a regular basis'. I know precisely what this is worth – we are back in the language and posturing of the Convention on International Parental Child Abduction, the fantasy world of international instruments where words are routinely mistaken for substantive actions.

Abstraction and caveat are persistent themes, undermining every bolder and more positive statement. We are told that the child shall have the right to freedom of expression, but only under restrictions regarding the undefined 'rights or reputations of others' or with regard to national security or public morals. We are told that the child shall have freedom of thought, conscience and religion. A child's religion – whose religion would that be, do you think? The very next line tells us that the parents' right to 'direct' these matters will be respected. Direction, then, rather than freedom and certainly no talk of freedom *from* religion. This clause, along with talk of identity and national values in Articles 8 and 29 comes closest to being actually retrograde. In a document intended to strengthen the hand of the child in an adult world, it is the adult addiction to domineering that has slithered into the garden and had its predictable say. The result is of little practical use for the thoughtful child in fending off attacks on his independence from madrasa, yeshiva, Our Lady of the Rosary Elementary or the Kim Jong-Il Children's Palace – no freedom to dump the treasured trash that held back the last generation, but instead the expectation that the child will be laden with the same old burden (aka national values) and all this passed off as care rather than control.

Perhaps we shouldn't be surprised that a Convention on the Rights of the Child has ended up reinforcing the authority of adults to give a sharp jerk on the cultural leash to any child who exercises their rights a little too much. It was, after all, drafted by adults. If it had been negotiated not by the real United Nations, but by a model United Nations staffed by representatives from the world's children, it would have been a very different document. Of course, back in the world of practicalities, we would have to admit that this more authentic charter, far from being acceptable to every country in the world, would be so radical in its demands that it would not be acceptable to any of them.

The Convention follows a general pattern in which much that is offered to the child by the adult world in policy terms imposes no direct cost on adults. The one great exception to this is the enormous cost of publicly funded education systems. Excellent though they are, the discourse by which taxpayers' support is maintained for such extravagance typically has much to do with control, the inculcation of national and religious values and the enhancement of pupils' usefulness to future employers rather than child rights. 'Pay your taxes so that your son or daughter can come home and more articulately contradict all your stuffy old ideas' will never really be a winner. Adults pay for education because it is

attuned to an adult agenda — the moulding of a new
generation into a comfortably familiar form. In this sense —
education as drag anchor — it hardly counts as a transfer of
resources at all.

An initiative can be costly without necessarily being a
good idea but the willingness to bear cost is a reliable indi-
cator of sincerity. Recent minor developments in the United
Kingdom as it adjusts to economic difficulties cast doubt on
that willingness. While a Child Trust Fund scheme which
placed funds under the control of children has been abol-
ished, the much more substantial Child Benefit paid out to
adults has been retained for most people at the same rate as
before. Child Benefit is really Parent Benefit and they can
spend it on anything they like for it is also parent voter
benefit. If the values of the more persuasive articles of the
Convention on the Rights of the Child were closer to being
realised, we would be having different debates and making
different choices. We would be debating whether a child in
respect of whom Child Benefit is being paid should, at the age
of fourteen or so, have half the benefit paid to them directly
as a mark of respect for their growing independence and a
recognition of their status as legitimate recipients of society's
redistributed wealth. The money would not all be wisely
spent, but that is true of money given to adult recipients as
well. Some of it would be more wisely spent than under the
current arrangements.

Can you imagine campaigning for such a proposal? The
words 'lead' and 'balloon' immediately come to mind and it
must be doubtful whether one could muster a single vote.
This could be down to the merits or the demerits of the case,

but could surely be more fully explained by the fact that all voters are adults and that none is a child. We all like to talk a good story about child rights – who would dare not to? – but when it comes to direct transfers from the adult to the child generation an irreducible stinginess sets in which derives from the fact that children don't have anything we want in material negotiations – they control no resources (as un-unionised workers in developing countries they don't even control their own labour), and they have no votes. On this the Convention on the Rights of the Child has nothing at all to say. It excludes the issue of political rights and by defining 'child' as a person below the age of eighteen, the most common voting age, reinforces the idea of the child as a politically silent person – a status previously shared by women or any of a range of racial and religious minorities not in favour with the political elites of the day. We have moved forward on those other fronts, but being a child remains synonymous with being politically voiceless. If we were serious about changing things, this is what we would change.

Votes for children should be an easy idea to dismiss – let's have a go. The most common objection and one always popular with older folks is that below a certain age people can't be expected to know enough to make an informed choice. The problem with this is that many adult voters have no more reliable or lucid grasp of the issues than an infant and make their choices on thoroughly non-rational grounds, especially if they are part of the core vote of left or right and act out of habit or identity. If expertise in public administration, economics and international affairs were to be a requirement for voting then we would immediately have to revise the electoral rolls, striking out many a middle-aged moron and bringing in a sizeable number of engaged and intelligent juveniles. This would probably improve the quality of decision-making, but can never be practical politics. Human nature being what it is, the procedure for deciding who is smart enough to vote would quickly be corrupted and before long 'smart enough to vote' would be redefined as 'people who think like me'. Besides, the intelligent can never be trusted to treat their intellectual inferiors fairly — they despise them too much. Crude as it may be, voting qualification will have to remain a matter of age — but what age, and why?

Voting at eighteen is now such a widely spread norm that many people feel that it must have an objective rational underpinning, that it must be written in tablets of logical stone. The truth is that the voting age has been mobile and arbitrary throughout the modern political era. In the United Kingdom in the early twentieth century it was twenty-one, unless you were female in which case it was nothing at all or, after 1918, thirty so your husband would have time to train you how to do it properly. The age was equalised in 1928 and reduced to eighteen in 1969. In the United States the voting age descended from twenty-one to eighteen only in 1971, largely because the expenditure of so much sub-twenty-one-year-old life in the Vietnam War was becoming awkward. This was a demand from Isaac to be heard in the counsels of Abraham. These examples are part of a consistent worldwide pattern in which the tablets of stone used to say twenty-one and were then broken and discarded in the late sixties and early seventies in favour of new tablets that say eighteen. We were stuck on twenty-one for a long time and it seemed as if it would always be that way. Now we have been stuck on eighteen for forty years, but we remember that things can change, if only we want them to.

In many countries serious people are gathering around a new reforming consensus that says the voting age should be reduced to sixteen. Austria, commendably, has already achieved this and is sure to be joined by others over the next few years as the new standard establishes itself. But at the level of mere argument there's a problem with sixteen and it's exactly the same as the problem with eighteen and with twenty-one – they are all arbitrary. If eighteen is acceptable, then seventeen can't be too bad. Indeed, North Korea has already shown the way with a voting age of seventeen, though it's too early to tell how this will affect the outcome of elections there. If seventeen brings no great disaster then one more short hop to sixteen begins to look like a modest reform. But there's no reason why we shouldn't ask the question again. Recent reports suggest that the sky has not fallen in on Austria and so a barely noticeable further nudge down to fifteen would hardly be revolutionary. And once you've got there, the fourteen-year-old school debating champion is going to be very hard to deal with if she thinks she also should have a say in society. In short, it's a continuum problem. In its logical structure it's the same as that most famous continuum problem in practical ethics, the abortion limit – the problem of where to draw a line when one position looks pretty much as good as another closely located beside it. I might note in passing the curious fact that religious conservatives do not campaign for the zygote vote in spite of asserting the full humanity of this object in all other respects. Presumably they want the opportunity to indoctrinate it first.

How do you get out of a continuum problem and its classic sterile exchange of assertions, no one of which can be more or less persuasive than another? You need an external principle, a breaker of the deadlock from outside the argument. And to find that we need to return to the issue of why anyone should have a vote at all. Historically and still today it's all about the money – there is an identification of the voter with the taxpayer, two groups that come together in the resounding old phrase 'no taxation without representation'. But there are other ways in which the state burdens the individual. Some have nothing to do with money, and some are very onerous. It burdens the individual through its laws and the punishments it imposes for breaking these laws. Mindful of this, we could make a tiny adjustment to our thinking about voting and march down the street behind a banner that says No Punishment Without Representation. Eventually we win the argument and the voting age is harmonised with the age of criminal responsibility: we live in a society where the state can't both punish you and ignore you. Wouldn't that feel better?

I'm pleased to say that in the United Kingdom this rationalisation of the franchise would reduce the voting age to ten – an excellent idea. What would this new Britain be like? I don't suppose there would be any great revolution. For one thing, very few ten-year-olds would actually vote; few eighteen-year-olds vote now. But it would feel very different, and this sense of renewal and change would only strengthen as time went on – it's the great power of symbolism in politics. Imagine it: election day comes and there you are, looking down on the child ahead of you in the queue.

'Oy,' you say to him, 'what are you doing here, sonny?'

He turns round to have a look and notices that you're over thirty.

'Get with the times, Grandad. I've got as much right to be here as you have. What do you think this is?'

He shows you his polling card. It looks just like the one accidentally issued to a fourteen-year-old at the last general election, only this one is not a mistake. It calls him one of 'the people' and is the first item of mail he has ever received in his own name. He was looking out for it because at primary school they have been learning all about the new rules.

Our new voter gets a ballot paper and stands on the box provided so he can reach the pencil stub with a piece of string taped to the end of it. He looks down the list of candidates. He's never heard of most of them and has no idea what they stand for, just like the grown-up voter in the next booth. He thinks the Labour Party sounds like hard work and his dad says Tories are scum. Parental influence would be exercised, but then it already is, often by parents decades dead, still lording it over the fixed ideas of their grown-up, core voter children. This new addition to the electorate would certainly not be any worse than them. He thinks about the people who have come to his school over the last two or three weeks. Some even came when there weren't any television cameras and we know what that means – this is a marginal constituency. Some of them seemed pleased to be there, others were distant and reluctant but came anyway because unlike talk about child rights this reform would result in a small but real transfer of power. They came because they had to.

The new voter can't remember much of what they said. They were a dull lot and did little to engage his current enthusiasms for squirrels, birds and the trees they live in — especially the ones in the nearby park which someone wants to bulldoze and build on. He understands what one candidate said about money being short and the land being valuable. He also remembers there was someone else who said green spaces in towns were important and that if people cared about these things they would find the money another way and the park and its trees with the squirrels and the birds would all still be there. He's forgotten her name, but she wore a badge on her jacket with a little picture and he sees the same picture on the ballot paper. He makes a cross beside it the way his teacher showed him and then skips down off the box to cast what will be, by the standards of the day, by no means the least informed vote.

In the early hours of the morning one person becomes a law-maker and the others fail. It has been a tight race and the winning majority, while not a single vote, is not a whole lot more. As the new parliament assembles at least one member must be aware that she might not have been there without the support of the younger voter. This could only be a forward step in our political arrangements. The moral stringency of the young, their firm unwillingness to accept that promises can be broken and unfairness explained away with lies they have not yet been trained to accept would surely not result in the politics of modern democracies getting any worse.

*

A more radical approach to the problems of the child in the adult world, and one that has an admirable logic, is that the child in question should not exist, or at least not in excessive numbers or in any excessively inconvenient way. This solves everything at a stroke and no doubt many of the suffering and deprived beings brought into existence in the world's most overcrowded slums would have been better off left as senseless raw material. Saying so merely indicates the benefits of contraception, which needs no defence.

In a depressed, anxious and solipsistic age, uncertain of its future these ideas have gained a new attraction for some. Third-world arguments have been imported to cast a generous light on first-world infertility with talk across the dinner tables of resources, water wars, sustainability, the sacrifice to greenness of the unconceived child. But all this can be brushed aside by pointing out that it may refer only to expansionary reproduction, not to replacement-rate reproduction and so not at all to the choice between being a parent and deliberate childlessness. Whatever is said, the choice of childlessness in developed societies cannot be explained by an altruistic desire to build a world fit for whales – especially when such a person celebrates their freedom by consuming for two, or three. It's not about the whales, it's about ourselves and the individualist's fear of the child as a threat to their dreams of self-fulfilment – an ideal that in most cases, surely, turns out not to have been a cause worth fighting for. Commerce encourages from behind, driving the unencumbered employee on towards the gilded carrot until it is too late, or until one finally learns to love Big Brother Inc. and agree that this really is as good as it gets.

Amongst my own sort – a breed more than ordinarily given to delusions of self-worth – there is a variation on this isolating search for freedom whereby one frets obsessively that being a parent will steal away one's creative energies and replace them with the less fragrant mundanities of life. In dreams the images are confused, but all ugly – the child as parasite, the child as cuckoo, the child as thief of our best and most golden self which dissolves and is replaced, as the dream pitches up to its screaming climax, with a vomit-spattered drudge who can't even remember what he once wanted to be. Our language hints at this with the word plagiarism: its original meaning is kidnapper, stealer of children. Its modern usage is a metaphor, a sort of joke no one gets any more about the pretentiousness of artists who regard the abduction of one of their sculptures or drawings, one of their little poems or the unattributed repetition of their witticisms as amongst the very worst of crimes.

To the unreproductive intellectual, the arrival of a child risks the kidnapping of their talent. It was the failed novelist and book reviewer Cyril Connolly who most pithily expressed this conviction with the phrase, 'there is no more sombre enemy of good art than the pram in the hall.' Sadly, it was this *bon mot* that turned out to be Connolly's most enduring creation – he was a high-functioning mediocrity at best and his meticulous use of prophylaxis did nothing at all to raise his creative standards. Had his house seethed with new life he might have achieved rather more, notwithstanding the inevitable attacks on his peace and quiet. Failing that, he would at least have had something better to do. In the end, he did — succumbing to fatherhood late in the day, acquiring a daughter at the age of fifty-six and a son at sixty-five. In his biography it is the images of these children that charmingly illuminate an otherwise gloomy narrative of a life that never quite began. In the most poignant it is a very old man who sits beside a small, white-haired boy, much of whose life he will never see. Connolly's expression is one of slack resignation to the fact that he has lived the wrong way round and that nothing can be done about it now.

For my part I am doubtful that a single preservable phrase was ever lost to childish interruptions, be they the urgent need to approve the latest picture, singing the alphabet along with the computer's range of comical robot voices, or allowing Makoto to sit on me and practise his three-year-old typing skills so that the sentence which starts like this one ends up more like slfjskilsu l;s;srihjg;--sorjfjs ggg lllllll33 — an improvement on my usual style, in the opinion of some critics. These are not obstructions to art — they are the reasons for it. More than that, they are its very sources and it has long seemed plausible to me that Tolstoy's magnificent fertility explained his superiority as a writer over the niggardly and misanthropic Dostoyevsky whose relative reproductive misfortune — two survivals from four late births — did little to relieve a morose and God-ridden nature. As for Henry James, few could doubt that getting to grips with a well-filled nappy could only have improved his work; at the very least, such domestic duties would have reduced its volume and in James's case that would have been an improvement. Philip Larkin was amongst the few to make good art out of voluntary childlessness, though he ran out of things to say long before the end, his non-existent offspring offering no growth and no change, just the predictable revelation that the promise of sterility turns out to be the most desolate of all.

I can't say what it feels like to have one of my books stolen. Perhaps it was Tomoko who came closest to giving me some insight into this. When the suicide threats ran into the sand she changed tactics to threatening my work instead. There she is, in a vivid mental snapshot, holding a laptop over her head and preparing to smash it on the floor – a shrieking, midget Hedda Gabler forever teasing the manuscript with the fire. When she graduated at the end to stealing the real children it was no compensation to have more time to spend writing a novel.

*

I take a break and head into the city. Late in the afternoon I find a table outside and install myself there to watch the early twenty-first century go by. My working mind is ninety years in the past, writing about failed idealists trying to stop a war. Simultaneously, much and nothing has changed. There's a malfunction by which I see things motionless and monochrome before a car horn or the waiter asking for my order jogs the stuttering machine and the world jerks into colour and movement. The hats have gone, and the moustaches mostly. The taxis have been updated, rounded, though they retain a strong family resemblance to their ancestors. In the colour version people make phone calls while walking in the street, but when a young man goes by with flowers wrapped in a cone of paper I feel drawn back to the old black and white past. Something else connects the two – the old photographs of municipal parks and promenades at coastal resorts are always well supplied with children and on this day, as I watch from my café table, there is almost the same spread of ages in the busy streets. But I know this is a distorted and temporary demographic – it's summer and the schools are on holiday, the cloisters have been broken open across all the low-fertility cities of the developed world. Briefly, it does seem like an earlier society and to my hopelessly subjective eye everyone appears a little happier, a little more hopeful in our always ageing, always more adult world.

It's boom time, mid-2004, and no one can guess at what is to come. The money is obvious, sticking up against the sky in the form of tower cranes. Three are visible from where I sit, leaning over various construction sites. From the hoardings around the nearest I can see that it is not offices they are building but homes or, as they prefer, executive living in the heart of the city. There is a picture of a dream couple in their pyjamas – they are in the bedroom, a glowing cell of gold and white, frozen in the eternal pre-sex pillow fight so adored by advertisers. She's just about to biff him with some Siberian goose down in an explicitly come-and-get-me manner and we know that as soon as the camera shutter has closed they are going to fall back on the organic Egyptian cotton sheets

and executively consummate their new flat. Who wouldn't
want it? Few of us, apparently – because in spite of the miserable square footage confessed in the lower right-hand corner
of the board, there's already a boastful sash across the lovers
that says SOLD OUT, that beautiful English phrase that only
ever has one meaning to the eternal salesman in us all.
Presumably precautions will be taken. If not, our pillow-
fighting couple will have to be on the move again before too
long because this development is strictly studio and one
bedroom.

If that's not a problem, I know from my wanderings that
they won't have to go far to skip from one living solution to
another – one of the cranes is building retirement apartments only a couple of streets away. Alarmingly, the entrance
qualification is anything over fifty years of age. This admits
one to a high security environment of luxury, convenience
and guaranteed childlessness: juvenile relatives may visit, but
not stay overnight. These grown-ups can have the grown-up
world all to themselves. The pitch on this hoarding is a little
different – a portly, retro-uniformed character who might
once have been Buttons the bellboy stands erect with one
hand behind his back, gesturing with the other towards a
warmly lit vestibule. It's the hidden hand that absorbs my
attention. I can't help suspecting that this smiling concierge
of the *après-vie* is hiding a large bunch of keys and that he, or
some other less definable force, would ensure that anyone
unwise enough to accept his invitation would never see the
outside of Catheter Mansions again.

I order another cappuccino as I connect these two buildings in my mind with a third I know of, a couple of miles

away down the hill in the city's cheap seats, by the tower blocks and the docks. This is my part of town and just across the road there is an anonymous, low-rise structure that completes the trinity. There is no signage at all, not even a name on the door: it is clearly not a place to which any casual visitor would need to find their way. This door, for all I know, might not work at all for I have never seen anyone enter or leave by it. Even the wheelchair-accessible ramp and the abundance of handrails are not really necessary. The staff go in the back way, where the vans with blacked-out windows come, stay half an hour, and head off in the direction of one of the many conveniently located funeral directors. The hearses are followed by a single limousine – empty, of course, save for the driver and an official mourner who will appear later on the invoice, itemised at an hourly rate.

These three buildings are really one, and I realise as I watch the life in a happier part of town that, of all the things I can see, this one, the block of flats, is the newest. It is an unprecedented domestic architecture for a wholly new society. From the hearths of Skara Brae through the teeming tenements of Rome and later cities, down even to the inter-war and post-war four- and five-bedroom detached villas of the middle classes, we have never lived in anything remotely like this. Those last buildings, with their garden grounds and privet hedges, separated themselves from each other. One of them was the scene of my childhood – a brief period in which the process of fragmentation seemed to slow or even stop a while before moving on at a greater pace, cutting into those nuclear units, subdividing them. Some of the reasons are positive, democratic: the small back bedroom that was once for the kitchen maid is no longer necessary, and quite right too. But we all know that's only part of the story. We are told that these new micro-dwellings, seen before only in the anchorite's cell, are a response to demand. But people can demand things because they are forced into them, not because they truly want them and we can't be sure whether this is the architecture of freedom or loneliness.

The copy in the developers' brochures does not allow for doubt and the photographs confirm it — endless images of saturated bliss against backgrounds of autumn foliage. It is as if the pessimism of Pascal — that human misery was largely attributable to people not knowing how to sit still in a room on their own — has become a mainstream opinion and that all that held us in more communal lifestyles in the past was a lack of resources. Now that we can afford atomisation why should we not indulge ourselves? This is a peculiarly first-world definition of freedom, long since emptied of political significance. It achieves its supreme expression in the privilege of masturbating in front of the television in a one-bedroomed flat whenever you feel like it because there's never anyone else there to tell you not to.

I pay my bill and wander home. These buildings and the world conjured in the advertisements and the empty black limousine with which it all ends come with me. Later, unable to sleep, I see the lights coming on and going off in the new architecture of freedom. Windows flicker as people move across them or adjust a blind, signalling. What does it mean, what's going on in there?

Across all the more prosperous cities of Britain, long-term partners are restless in their luxury urban living units.

Fortieth birthdays loom – they're not even faux-young any more. At three in the morning, each pretending to the other that they are still asleep, they go over the turning points of the last twenty years. They look more closely and find the small print no one warned them of at the time.

Something clarifies and he perceives himself at last as a particle of economic irony, a slave of the labour-saving machine. His rewards are for collaboration in the huge collective fouling of the nest that is growth economics. But what can he do? Everyone lies and no one has any better ideas. Outside, the dawn chorus of traffic starts earlier every year. What seemed like choices reveal themselves now as impositions, the tricks of a mindless system that has only its own perpetual expansion to aim at. Did some shill get commission for selling him this life? Is there a neck he could wring? His hands tighten at the thought, but the truth is he bought it without ever looking at the alternatives. He can't even say he put up a fight.

She works too, of course. How else could they afford it all? Down below, amidst the concrete piles that hold it all up, in their dedicated parking space, there stands a spotless mass of black metal and glass. This car is marketed as allowing the owner to drive straight to the top of a Scottish mountain, should he or she wish to do so. In its manufacturer's promotional literature it is always alone, the only car in the world. In reality, it is rarely more than ten metres from another vehicle. They bought it because of its low exhaust emissions. They bought the responsibility lifestyle, and the platinum in the car's catalytic converter. They paid their share to the mines in the third-world countries that spend the lives of four or five of their workers every month in cost-efficient accidents and flush the waste from their separating plants into the once-living rivers. They're not stupid. They know that when one man gets clean he pulls the plug and someone else gets dirty. But they are clean.

She checks the clock and thinks of her mid-morning meeting — six and a half hours to go. That damned car — why can she not get it out of her mind when she has so many other things to worry about? She tries to think ahead, to plan out the next, and professionally most rewarding decade. Where will she be by the end of it? Her inner life is a job interview.

It doesn't work. She is pulled back to the past when decisions were made with no thought for the future. Small moments, moments in the bedroom no one else would ever know about, when the course of another life was dammed up and held back, for another few months at least.

Her period is late. She says 'late' in her mind, but it has missed altogether. Her friend, yesterday at a half-hour lunch snatched away from the office, started to congratulate her, to bounce with excitement and happiness in her chair. She had to stop her right away. That wasn't it at all. That was impossible. They agreed it was just a one-off — a little holiday, they joked.

She moves her hand down below the covers, over a smooth, unmarked belly and under the waistband of her pyjamas. She looks at the clock and strains to avoid the unavoidable thought. Perhaps she was just run down.

The car intrudes again. The dangerous part comes straight to the surface, too quick for her to do anything about it. It is page 95 of the owner's manual: How to Install a Child Safety Seat. There are numbers and red arrows pointing to the important parts of the simple line drawing. A figure, female of course, leans over to secure a strap. In the seat there is a child of two and half, or three perhaps – she isn't good at guessing ages. The position of the little body is accurately outlined but the face, beneath the hairline (it seems to be a boy) is left quite blank. It could be anyone's child. Perfect, fragile, protected – hers?

The drawing is too much. The muscles of her abdomen convulse under her hand. Hot tears trickle back over her temples and collect uncomfortably in her ears. She wants to sniff loudly, but worries that he isn't really asleep and doesn't want to give herself away. Briefly, she thinks of getting out of bed, pulling on some clothes and going down to the lower parking level just to sit in the car and get the manual out of the glove compartment and look at the drawing and then at the back seat where the blank-faced child would be. With a drowsy, half dreaming start of fear the child becomes real, has been waiting there for hours, forgotten. She runs towards the vehicle. She tries to control the dream, to direct the scene so that she arrives to find an unharmed sleeping boy. But the vision sidesteps and vanishes. She is in bed again and it is all right – there is no forgotten child, she is not needed.

She is a partner specialising in intellectual property law. She is five hundred pounds an hour. She is a modern Queen Midas, run to ground, unable to touch anything she truly loves. Can't she give it back? Cast off the fatal spell? Daylight shows beneath the curtains, calling her to the business day.

Beside her lies a man. Perhaps she is wrong, but she feels

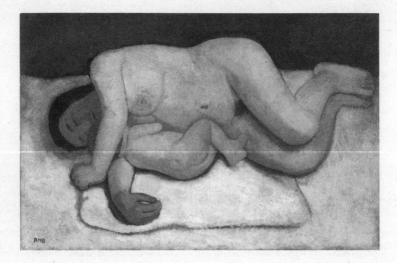

sure there must be a growing resentment there, building to something worse, because of everything she hasn't given him. He is a provider only for himself, and that can't be enough. Lately, he has been less happy, but never says what the problem is.

She shakes her head – the whole thing doesn't bear thinking about. It's nonsense, just a mood. Obsessive and irrational when she has so much. That old word comes to her, the one that meant more to her mother's generation, her grandmother's even. Would she be ungrateful for this victory, so long fought for?

Yes, she is emancipated. These days we would say they both are – but from what?

7　Hatred

When I think of myself as a murderer I am suffused with a deep sense of peace. There I am in my mind, lying back on my prison cell bed with the thought of the deceased hate-object easing through my veins as the smoke of fine cigars was always supposed to do in old-fashioned adverts. I smile, involuntarily, and have to make an effort not to laugh out loud. The crime endures for me as a physical as well as a mental delight – a moveable feast of vengeance and cleansing as easily savoured inside a prison cell as outside. In this sense I am unpunishable. The proceeds of my crime are joy and they can never be seized by any state. Again and again the images and sensations unspool – the last pulse of the constricted arteries in the neck, the last bubbles rising gently from nostrils and mouth to the water's surface, the bloodied hand falling away from the telephone, unable to call the ambulance which could not, in any case, arrive in time. The pleasure revives, almost as fresh as in the act itself: colours are more intense, sounds clearer and more harmonious, the world generally a more tolerable place for no longer being shared with the one unacceptable person. The resulting prison sentence presents itself as part of a well-struck bargain. Indeed, the years of incarceration hardly seem long enough to extract the full satisfaction arising from what the judge so shallowly describes as my 'appalling' actions – a meaningless cliché of disapproval.

The newspapers report that Galbraith showed no emotion when he was sentenced. This is not quite right. There was an emotion – one of mild puzzlement as I scrutinised the judge. I have to struggle to follow his words, as is normal when those two strangers, the lucky man and the unlucky man, encounter one another. He is reaching for the big phrases – something booming and faintly metrical to express a whole society's contempt. It's not working. As drama the trial fails completely and I am committed to a life of imprisonment as feebly as Derek from bathroom fittings is summoned to checkout 15. He should have got me to do it for him: I would, inevitably, have done a better job. And what is it, precisely, that I find puzzling? The simple question of how two members of the same species could have come so totally to misunderstand each other. That is my vision of the solemn proceedings – not a trial, but a dark costume comedy, the theme of which is mutual incomprehension.

Some will understand these remarks, others will shrink from them in disgust, others still will understand them privately but feign ignorance or outrage in public, or will respond with the fake rhetoric of forgiveness, trusting too much in its power to dispel an uncomfortable reality. What this suggests to me is that in the field of hatred we find one of humanity's great conceptual divides and it is no matter of mere ideas. Those who know hatred really are different from those who do not – not just in their opinions, but deep in themselves.

Circumstance dictates which of these conditions we fall into. Some are born under hatred's flag, learning by six, seven or eight to hate all the folks their relatives hate; to be afraid

— as the song has it — of people whose eyes are oddly made. Others live free and clear, safely beyond hatred's reach until sideswiped by a moral collision, the driver that jumps the lights, the aircraft heading for your office window as you look up from your morning coffee. Choice is not possible, but if it were would it be wholly artificial to ask which would be the better course — a cheerful but vulnerable ignorance of hatred, or a gloomy knowledge which might guide us in a crisis to a less disastrous or ineffective decision? It's a strange question and I suspect one must have travelled in hatred's country even to think of it. My answer, with regret, is that those who understand hatred have a better understanding of the world. There is one essential proviso: that having travelled, one must then find one's way home.

*

How should we proceed with such a very odd enquiry? While we are content to learn about love by experiencing it, no one would willingly choose the same direct route to a knowledge of hatred. The happy and fortunate life remains ignorant of these feelings, almost by definition, and it would require an abnormal degree of commitment to want to induce a state of hatred in oneself out of scientific curiosity. There is an analogy in the distinguished tradition of the medical self-experimenter — those who martyr their arms to the mosquito or gulp down pathogens to find out how best to deal with the consequences. Much of what we know about poisons must first have been learned by tasting them and this Russian roulette quality would probably be carried across to an over-bold investigation of hatred. The experimenter would not die entirely, but a part of him might well do so, and we know from our observations of hatred in others that the worst cases lead to a lifelong moral and intellectual disablement.

Some risk management is needed. A journey into hatred, if such a thing is possible at all, should be an imaginative one that draws on the work of those who see more clearly than we do, whose minds are still intimately available through the art and literature they have heaped up over the generations, the non-digital Second Life that offers a brush with the most alarming experiences and a good chance of still coming away at the end, more or less undamaged.

The literature of hatred is not great, especially if one takes the phrase to mean writing of a sufficient quality, writing which attempts to understand rather than merely to express hatred, which literature never does. By literature of hatred I mean, for example, the literature of nationalism as opposed to the waving of flags and the scattering of enemies, the literature of dogs as opposed to the sound of barking. The latter is common enough, but always ephemeral − it may be powerful to those attuned to it, but these things always wither as active images or narratives as soon as the fashion changes. The Horst Wessel Song was belted out with enthusiasm and sincerity in the Germany of the 1930s, but on the inner life of the singers it is completely mute and it will not, I think, be appearing in any poetry anthologies between now and the end of the world. Its contemporary equivalents − the white supremacist website or the Islamist suicide bomber's goodbye video − cannot hope to have a longer lifespan. These expressions of hatred are too shallow and external to be of any help. We could observe and reproduce them well enough for a thriller or an action movie, but for a great performance, one summoned from within, something different is needed.

I'm doubtful that the contemporary creative scene can meet the required standard. In the English tradition the theme has arguably been in decline since the darkness and the distinctively sharp teeth of late Elizabethan and Jacobean theatre, and in modern work I find the emotion spread thinly across the surfaces of genre fiction and its filmic equivalents. The marionettes of the commercial author's imagination grimace or stab at each other, or cunningly drop poison in the spousal G&T without ever convincingly penetrating hatred as a deep and defining mode of life. In the end we find it was all done to fulfil a small man's plan to get away with a small man's swag — the life insurance payout, or keeping the clandestine affair on the road, or anything else that would never quite raise the creaking mechanics of the plot to the level of tragedy, let alone the bitterness of real life.

One suspects that it is not merely lack of ability in these writers that produces such psychologically colourless results; even if they could go further they would hold back for fear that it might not be wise to do so, that an indecency would result which could only revolt a refined readership. More than that, if it were done well it would reveal a knowledge in the author that many now hold to be deplorable in itself. We have lost touch with hatred — its remoteness is part of what we like about modern life, part of what we mean by civilisation, that etiolated, tender, glasshouse quality to our emotional lives that keeps order, internal and external.

Through the entertainment industry, as well as certain
forms of professional sport, the passions are exercisable as the
body is exercised on a running machine – an elaborate and
costly device created to make sure we never actually get
anywhere. And then, when there's a stabbing after the game
and the chap's dragged off and gets what he deserves we shake
our heads and say 'how terrible'. We are sincere enough and
have no desire to follow his example, but there's still a curiosity about what it must be like to go the whole way, to step
off the running machine and find ourselves rushing forward
through a suddenly brilliant reality. We don't want to do it,
but feel vaguely humiliated by the knowledge that we can't
even live as if we might do it. If we want to taste a little of this
intensity through the life of the mind, it's not at all clear
where we should go.

The same is true of the visual arts – the icons of hatred are
often poor stuff. The street furniture of socialist realism and
Arno Breker's oddly similar fascist men of steel are largely in
storage now, or in scrapyards waiting to be melted down.
They weren't art at all, just obedience, and they died with
their masters. If they attract the attention of cultural historians in the future, the fact that these scholars will often have
to work from photographs will be the proper measure of the
work's quality.

We find a graphic equivalent in the propaganda poster,
often impelled by hatred even when it is on the side of the
angels hating the bad guys. It's a confusing area in which we
find ourselves hampered by the contamination of our
aesthetic judgement by other values. We're sympathetic to
the image whose message we approve of, dismissive of the

other even though they might both be, as acts of communication, equally skilful. Sometimes we are torn. Riefenstahl still has her admirers; they apologise, then sheepishly go back to their admiration. This does get us a little closer to the insight I'm looking for — a brief and quickly repressed discovery that we too respond to hatred's mesmeric attractions. But in the end, propaganda just won't do. Unlike the fundamentals of human experience it exists too much in time. Picture yourself: having made the appointment with the archive, there you finally are, lifting the acid-free tissue guard from the treasured John Heartfield photograph or Spanish Civil War poster only to find, with a droop of the shoulders, that it has become that eternally disappointing object, a historical document. Its enemies are not your enemies — probably not anyone's any more. It's dead. If we want the real thing, the hard stuff of hate art that might just work as alternative experience, we must go up-market.

There is a small class of writers who might be able to help: those exhibiting the rare combination of high literary standards and an open taste for hatred. Knut Hamsun is one of these — the Nobel Prize winning novelist and ardent Hitler-lover who neatly expressed his values by sending the Nobel medallion to Joseph Goebbels (complaisant husband to the familicidal Magda), as a token of his high esteem. Shortly before making this gift he was a guest of the Goebbels family and was charmed by their six children, neatly lined up to be presented to the great man. After the war he could think only of a mechanical and passive metaphor with which to describe them. They were, he said to his psychiatrist, 'a row of organ pipes'. Hamsun hated pretty much everything that wasn't

Norwegian – and that is pretty much everything. The only exception to this were the Germans who humiliated Norway. Only the Nazis had something sufficiently attractive to draw him away from his bijou nationalism. Among those who really could write novels, and Hamsun could, he appears to be one of the go-to guys on the whole hatred thing. There's a handful of others like him, the most distinguished being the French writer Céline. Céline was one of the few Frenchmen to spend the last days of the Second World War heading away from his home country and towards Germany in hope of sanctuary. He was a friend of the talentless anti-humanist Breker and approvingly attached the name 'Hamsun' to a boat in one of his own novels. In the field of hatred he attained a degree of perfection by criticising Hitler – if only on the grounds that he was, in Céline's very private world, too Jewish. Seven years after his death Céline's house burned down but his parrot, Toto, survived. Suspecting arson – perhaps politically motivated – the police took the unusual step of interrogating the bird. Consistent to the last, Toto would only say that the Jews did it, but otherwise remained tight-beaked. A celebrated incident in its day, it gave rise to the widespread but unfair view that parrots have a limited capacity for independent thought. It's not the parrots that have the problem – it's their owners.

Suppose we put together an ad hoc anthology of the works of characters such as these – we might add a little Ezra Pound, a few of the more crassly anti-Semitic lines of T. S. Eliot – and then settle down for a good long mental marinade in its juices. When we're done and struggle back up to the light and clean air has anything been learned from this brief trip to the literary underworld? A few scraps around the edges perhaps, but about the thing itself in its simple, caustic essence, very little, or nothing at all. There are two reasons for this. The first is that these major creative intellects are big enough and complex enough to encompass the hatred and still have something left to produce a valid art. They are at their best when they are most distant from their hatreds, and at their weakest and least impressive when they are submitting to them, as if their ability shrivels and sickens the closer they get to this most dangerous of emotions. The other reason is more interesting: even when they are indulging themselves there is a ready-made and impersonal quality to their hatreds. However fine the style, the driving emotions themselves are second-rate. While these great writers writhed and chewed the carpet with rage at the thought of Semitic conspiracies, of the monstrous fertility of the racial other, of the menacing idiocy of everyone in the world but themselves, they were giving their minds up to other people's ideas, people who were very much their inferiors in most other respects. This is the great sin we find at what should have been the high points of their art — not their hatred, but their lack of originality. Arriving at these passages we experience not new knowledge, but merely embarrassment at having to witness such gruesome self-betrayals by minds we were once tempted to admire. We do learn one thing — that hatred in its purest form is always personal. Its pre-packaged versions, those that hand out uniforms and party cards are never the real thing. This is the Scout camp of hatred. What I'm after is the one man, or woman, wilderness expedition.

The morally comfortable suspect this is all a wild goose chase. In their world hatred is kryptonite to creativity, let alone to beauty and goodness. Where you find one there's just no point in looking for the other. But because moral self-confidence is often an illusion, the good man never passes up an opportunity to undermine it. A single example would do. Try this one.

It's a four-hundred-year-old picture of a couple of women cutting a man's head off. The subject was something of a commonplace in the art of the time – it is an illustration to the Bible story of Judith and Holofernes, a story that is about war and collective identities rather than, as might appear from the version above, men and women. Judith was seriously hot. She also loved God and the Jews and hated foreigners, especially the Assyrians who were besieging her town under the command of their general, Holofernes. She tricked her way into the general's company, cuddled up to him, kept refilling his glass and laughing at his feeble off-colour jokes. The poor fellow didn't stand a chance and as soon as he keeled over from all that booze she cut his head off and took it back home in a bag. What a girl.

When men tell this story, or paint it, it's about loyalties and turning the tables on the designated enemy. That's why their versions aren't much good; even Caravaggio's effort on the same subject lacks the energising viciousness of the image above.

We don't care about Assyrians today, but we do still look at this painting. We might walk briskly through a display of graphic clichés from a dilute and distant religious tradition, getting no answer to the repeated and perfectly fair question 'What is this to me?' But then we come across this image and it stops us in our tracks, whether we like it or not.

Even before peering at the gallery label we might guess that this is not a man's picture of a woman cutting a man's head off, but a woman's picture of the same thing. That changes everything. We might not know the real story behind this work, but I think it's possible to read something of it in the painting itself. It's not surprising to learn that the woman who created it, Artemisia Gentileschi, may have been a victim of rape herself and when the case came to court was very probably subjected to judicial torture by a patriarchal legal system that preferred its own version of the truth. Besides all that, she knew the daily economic and social injustice of being a talented woman artist in a man's world. She didn't care about Assyrian generals or Jewish national heroines any more than we do, and that is precisely why we still look at her picture more than we look at the others. Artemisia's version is about men and women, and justice, and hatred. It's also personal.

Does it work? Does it connect with the darkest extremes, tell us something that couldn't be articulated any other way? I believe it does. One can stand beside it in the Uffizi for a good long time, pretending to consult the guidebook but examining instead, with a discreet sidelong glance, the female visitors to the gallery. It does not speak to all of them, but in some there is an intensity, a close communing with the work followed by a slight and private smile that is exactly what one would expect from Judith herself the moment she reveals the blade she has been holding behind her back all this time. It is, at a deep level, a victim's painting. It is the product of many hundreds of hours of solitary concentration on the sharpness of the steel, the softness of the muscle and sinew parting before its edge, the texture and track of the blood as the vital vessels are cut, the grate of bone transmitted up the weapon's shaft as it first finds the vertebrae and then slips between them to complete the job. The least specific things about it are the features of Holofernes' face. We would recognise these women in the street, but he is just Bearded Man number 1. We might say, casually, that it could be anyone – not an Assyrian general at all, but someone you used to know, perhaps someone you trusted. It might be someone you still know. And now you're thinking about the knives in the kitchen drawer. And in a moment there you are, as bright and clear as in Artemisia's imagination, standing over the sleeping body, reaching out for a handful of that coarse black hair to get a tight grip for the task ahead. It's art therapy for grown-ups, a truly dangerous image that teeters on the edge of persuasive licence for the act itself. Go on, says Artemisia, the passionless daylight people say this is wrong, but you and I know different. Go on, do it. This is the test that it passes. This is what makes it a masterpiece not diminished by hatred as we mostly are, but illuminated and made great by it — a properly intense and honest hatred for what is properly hateful.

Artemisia's painting is a rarity, but not unique. The genuinely aesthetic expression of hatred does exist in literature as well. The strongest claim is made at the midpoint of literature's historical timeline when Dante took the obvious and never to be bettered step of privatising Hell itself and taking the whole place over for his own purposes. His *Divine Comedy* is a hefty triple-decker where the sturdiest construction is to be found on the lowest, infernal levels. Here the pleasures of the thought-murder ascend to a new and magnificently sadistic level. In this world death really is too good for them. This is where the headless Holofernes wakes, thinking 'Phew! At least the worst is over now', only to be met with a peal of dark laughter and an endless future.

The *Divine Comedy*'s most obvious lesson is circular, though by no means empty. What it tells us is that we have an innate relish for maintaining hells of the imagination and populating them with our hand-picked selection of inmates. Powerless as infants in the real world, our solution is to maintain a part of our minds where we sit atop our own private dictatorships, handing down unspeakable judgements from which there is never any appeal. It is an instance of art surrendering and sending us back to ourselves, to do what only we do best: patrol the smoking lava pits of our personal punishment chambers with our dainty goat feet and twitching arrowhead tails. There we look out for the familiar faces, nonchalantly reaching over with our trident to push them under again, where they belong — in the place we have reserved just for them, in the ninth and deepest circle of torment, the hell of the child-stealers. Naturally, in your version the details might be different.

The experience of reading the three, increasingly draining volumes of Dante's massive work delivers an unintended message. It is an accidental experiment in the most basic tastes of the human animal. We devour the *Inferno* with crude appetite, *Purgatory* is what you would expect from the title, *Paradise* is hell. Online sales figures are only the latest confirmation of what has been true about our species for all the seven centuries since the book's appearance, and will no doubt remain true for the indefinite future.

Knowledge of hatred does not, in the end, come from reading or viewing its imaginative expression. This only shows what is already there — a fact too ordinary and universal to need a masterly work of art to make it clear. What the few great pieces of hate art tell us is enormously important, but also enormously simple: to stop lying about our emotions. This accounts for the enticing quality of their invitation — they beckon us down the steps, and then down again into the warmth and fire-light of the sub-basement bar, into the society of friends and fellow-sufferers where we can live honestly and so little needs explaining, or hiding. Above the dingy rainbow bottles, by the stopped clock and the useless calendar there is a faded print of a four-hundred-year-old painting. We raise our glass as we drink each other's health in The Judith and Holofernes.

*

Enough of art. Let us consider instead an earthquake and a pair of tan socks. Imagine a news report playing on a television screen. It's from Japan, it's late in 2004 and the Chuetsu earthquake has just struck. The media are doing their usual thing — collapsed houses, emergency vehicles, people in hard hats and high visibility jackets, a large crack in the road to show what moved where. It's not my country, but it is my children's and so I ease off on the remote and follow it through.

Against a rubble backdrop two men are struggling with a stretcher. There's no hurry — we can see that the blanket over the body has been pulled up to cover the face. This has exposed the feet at the other end — two small, female feet wearing the aforementioned tan ankle socks. I am immediately excited by the potential significance of this corpse. I lean forward, my heart rate rises, I perspire, my pupils dilate to take in every promising detail of the socks and the two little feet they cover. My mind races to the conclusion that a dream has come true, that prayers have been answered. In my story, the feet appear like those of the Wicked Witch of the East at the start of *The Wizard of Oz* — the stripy stockinged remains of the enemy so justly and enjoyably crushed by Dorothy's house as it spins down from the tornado. Poetic justice allows the treasured magic slippers to be recovered; in the end they will answer every heart's desire.

There are no shoes on these Japanese feet — this has been an indoor demise — and I instantly convince myself that both they and the socks are familiar. In this upside-down identity parade these dead feet are the only suspect on offer and my hopelessly biased senses are certain it's a match. I am already thinking of the calls I must make to the British Consulate in Osaka, the air tickets I must reserve. I anticipate some difficulty in repossessing my children from Japanese social services — the state is also such a jealous parent — but I'll manage it somehow. A new and utterly transformed life is opening up, and it all starts with this happy moment.

I peer more closely at the screen and speak at last, eager to share my optimism with the others in the room.

'It looks like Tomoko!'

They are shocked, but not as much as I am by their reaction. Only now do I realise how little I have in common with these people, or ever will have. They have not changed, they still live without enemies and without hatred or insight into its part in other lives. I am the one who has changed — a new and different person who will have to watch what he says from now on whenever he is in the company of more tender, mainstream sensibilities. As for the earthquake, it turned out to be in the wrong part of Japan altogether. They were someone else's feet, sadly.

*

Although my new expertise in the subject of hatred had arrived as a result of wholly private events, it just so happened that the newsflow of the early twenty-first century was peculiarly in keeping with it. I seemed to have stumbled into a disconcerting, postmodern production in which the designer had colour-coordinated my inner life with the morning's newspaper and the evening TV bulletin. I doubt, in the long run, that we will recognise the lethal misunderstandings of Islam and the West as the answer to the question 'What happened between 2000 and 2010?' The right answer will have more to do with economics, technology, China, population growth and the environment. For those who lived through it, what happened between 2000 and 2010 was that we got distracted from what really mattered, and what distracted us was a story about hatred.

For almost all of us this was a screened experience and, as is usually the case in the screenplay world, the story starts when all is going well. In my case getting my hair cut in Reading on a sunny early afternoon in September. I have one of Tomoko's shopping lists in my pocket and when I'm done I'll go home to where my four- and two-year-old sons will be playing in the kitchen and perhaps do a little work on my second book. For early twenty-first-century westerners it's the pre-hatred world.

'The whole thing's collapsed,' says one barber to another.

'What do you mean?'

'It's gone. Just completely gone.'

I hear it, but it doesn't make sense – I'm still tuned to another station. It's the tone of their voices that gets through in the end. The ancient, doggy part of my brain finally wakes up and cocks an ear.

'What's that?'

Once I've identified the building in question I realise how extraordinary it is that it should have collapsed. I run through all the wrong answers – structural failure, very small earthquake that somehow affected only one building, some bloke left the gas on in the basement.

'A plane hit it?'

Well there you are – a freak air accident. Dreadful business.

'And the other one too? *Another* plane?'

Some time passes during which I am reading, in a metaphorical sense, *The Pet Goat* – which is exactly what George W. Bush was doing in the Emma E. Booker Elementary School in Sarasota County, Florida when he heard the same news. Criticism on this point has been hard to resist, though perhaps unfair – many of us spent some time reading *The Pet Goat* before catching up with this new reality, though not necessarily the full seven minutes required by the President of the United States. I give the haircut the hurry up and head for the entertainment section of the nearest department store. And there it is on fifty TV screens all at once. Now I believe it.

Being a modern man, a node in the global telecommunications brain, I believe myself to be an expert in all things. Accordingly, I make my first pronouncement to the astonished salesman standing beside me.

'They're going to make someone pay for this.'

As my predictions go it didn't turn out to be too bad – I just didn't anticipate the extent to which it would be the wrong people. That's the problem with the less personal, less discriminate type of hatred.

Why was this such a shocking event? Can it really have been the disaster-movie graphics cutting through to the jaded cinema-goer and computer-gamer one sunny morning? The distress of bystanders was recorded at many points and cannot be doubted, but what about months later when there still seemed to be something left under our collective skin – what accounts for that? It can't have been the numbers. The student of epidemics, earthquakes and Chinese floods knows that millions can be swept from the table at a stroke and it makes little difference to the broad outline of history. As I write we approach the first anniversary of the Haitian earthquake, an event that resulted in a death toll many times greater than that of the 9/11 attacks, but which we have not found many times more disturbing. Something else must be going on. If it isn't the images and it isn't the numbers, perhaps it's the motive? And yet the mere deliberateness of it can't provide much of an explanation either. Five to six times as many people are deliberately killed in the United States every year as a matter of that society's ordinary functioning. Few believe that this calls for any major policy changes and some point to it as a price worth paying for more general freedoms. If the 9/11 attacks were just a third-quarter statistical blip in the background murder rate, why all the fuss? Could it be hatred's re-emergence on a grand scale into the midst of a complacent existence that had variously denied, explained away or forgotten this element of our common nature? We know the scene well. The hero and heroine have finally killed it off, whatever it was. It's had five comebacks in the last twenty minutes, but this time they've really done it in. Breathless, bloodied, the improbable but

morally reassuring victors embrace. They position for the
kiss of the happy future as it rises stealthily from the swamp
at their backs, more ghastly than ever. When you thought
you were the happy couple, and it turns out not to be a movie
at all – that's when it sticks under the skin. But how did it
come as such a surprise?

In our public affairs, in the rich and stable world at least,
hatred went into a downturn in 1946 when the sentences of
the Nuremberg trials were carried out and we moved forward
to the sunlit uplands of 'post-war', a period partly defined by
its bridled emotions. Since then we have been required to
analyse even the most vicious conflicts as problems rather
than as passions, and the public figure who admits any
insight into the emotions of the terrorist or the suicide
bomber abruptly shortens their own career. A minor but
typical example came with the fall from grace in January 2004
of the British politician Jenny Tonge. Commenting on the
living conditions of the Palestinians in the Gaza Strip, she
declared that if she had to live like that she 'might just
consider' becoming a suicide bomber herself. She was given
the usual opportunity publicly to denounce her own convictions but declined, choosing instead to explain her remarks
by saying that, given the violence, provocation and humiliation suffered by the Palestinan people – as she put it – she
could 'understand' the extreme response of suicide bombing.
It appears to have been the use of the word 'understand'
which sealed her fate and she was promptly sacked from her
front bench position. The idea that understanding is a vice is
an unusual one, especially among politicians who ordinarily
display great reluctance to admit not knowing the answer to

any question. The episode confirmed the unique status that hatred has acquired: it is the one field of human experience in which the wise man, or the man who would be thought wise, must proclaim his ignorance rather than his knowledge.

This diminished appetite for hatred – for enquiring into it, let alone for the exploratory thrill-seeking of getting close to it – reached its final point at a particularly inconvenient moment and not, I think, by coincidence. For the transaction of 11 September 2001, some degree of co-operation was needed between the two parties – for one to be madly awake, and the other to have lulled themselves to sleep. This explains the event's exceptional psychological impact – it involved the reassertion of old truths about human nature which, precisely because they had been forgotten, arrived with the force of something new.

I can't recall how much of this I thought at the time. However important, 9/11 was still an external event. The darker aspects of current affairs were one line on the graph, private life another. It would take twenty months or so before these lines crossed, before I came home to find all that I cared for gone, destroyed by a deliberate and long-planned action. It would be from then that I started to see everything differently, everything as connected.

The scale is, admittedly, a little different. Then again, we are apt to make grand comparisons in our domestic lives – one man's compromise on whose turn it is to empty the bin is another man's retreat from Moscow. There you are, staggering out with the stinking sack, the putrid burden of defeat, muttering under your breath about how it starts like this but ends at Water-bloody-loo. An exaggeration mis-measures the world, but in other respects does not necessarily get it wrong. More and more I see the private in the public, the public in the private. It is no surprise to wake to find the razor wire uncoiled down the centre of the bed, or a makeshift wall being built where once was a street, or a corridor between two rooms in the home of a seceding family. Talk becomes rhetoric. I become a keen student of barriers, of all that raises up divisions of fact and sentiment.

After the abduction of my children I am with those who stand at Panmunjom, waiting powerlessly for the planets to align, for the once in a decade breach in the Korean ceasefire line. 'How are you? I could only see you in dreams.' She embraces her daughter who is herself an old woman. Kim is ninety-six years old. I marvel at the stamina of this cruelty, and at the stamina of the forces arrayed against it. After three days they are parted again, the curtain drawn back across their lives.

A more frequent story at this time is Israel and Palestine and the construction of the latest of history's walls, the West Bank separation barrier. This is an irresistible analogy for a failing cross-cultural family – the perpetually hate-fuelled pre-divorcees never getting away from each other because they can't even agree on who gets what part of the house, the children literally sick with fear, never helped by the monster-manipulators they have for parents. This is Dante's news story, straight from Hell. For me it's hardly a news story at all, just a domestic drama writ large. I see that everything here is a child. The map is a child, the bulldozed olive grove is a child, the apartment block in East Jerusalem is a child. Self is abandoned as everyone becomes territory. To give birth to a child is to give birth to territory.

Drifting through the photo gallery of early twenty-first-century hatred I always return to a single brief clip, the one where child and territory cease being metaphors and become a single, literal reality. It arises from the coming together of a news camera, some soldiers, a riot in the Gaza Strip in September 2000 and a father and his son caught in the middle. It's Jamal al-Durrah and his twelve-year-old son Muhammad in blue jeans and sandals. They are crouching against a cinder-block wall. There is gunfire, though we can't at first see where or from whom. Through the effect of the camera we seem to be very close. It is full daylight and the air is clear. The hands of these two people can be seen and hold no weapons. Muhammad is terrified, screaming with fear. He is trying to make himself small, burrowing into his father who has tight hold of him by the arm. Jamal is signalling frantically. These people are not hiding – they are doing the very opposite, drawing attention to themselves, pleading for a brief gap in the firing so they can run across the road and be safe. Then there is a sudden cloud of light grey dust around Jamal and his son as someone machine-guns them. Because they are against a wall we can see that the bullets do not hit the wall either to the left of the man and the boy, or to the right of them. The bullets only hit the wall after passing through their bodies. The two figures go still and the clip ends. Astonishingly, Jamal survived but his son, Muhammad, did not.

Predictably, the images themselves become a new piece of territory, bitterly fought over. Some seize on their usefulness as propaganda and they are later associated with further inexcusable acts of violence. Others declare their unreality. They resort to what we might call the 'Shanghai defence' — like the South Station baby bombed by the Japanese sixty-three years previously we are to believe what they say, not what we see. It simply never happened at all. It was a performance, a forgery, a work of art, perhaps a nightmare, anything but real. We would all wish for that to be true, though we all know it isn't. Standing outside the dispute, all I can say is that the contenders are yet to find the limits of their degradation.

This too I see differently either side of the changes in my own life, and in an unexpected way. Rerunning it in my mind — I no longer watch the images themselves — I find a more balanced view than I would previously have thought possible. I understand the acts of vengeance that these pictures promoted, but I surprise myself now by finding that I understand the soldier too. It is odd that those on one side of the al-Durrah debate have chosen always to lie about it rather than offer a defence, for there surely is a defence. It must lie in the whole life history of the soldier, right down to that day at the Netzarim junction, the story of the forces that made him what he was. It lies in the weight of the uniform on his back, how its insignia press in upon his conscience. It lies in all that he was made to believe, in everything that worked to make that other, artifical man, the one that lives just inside his more human skin — the obedient and patriotic mechanism that reaches down the sinews of the arm, takes aim at a future enemy, and pulls the trigger. This is a strong defence, a story of how an idea works to strip away a man's freedom piece by piece, and his responsibility too.

And if the idea that in the world of hatred the personal and the political are really one asks too much of your waking mind, let me press the button on the remote one last time. It's still the news — is it the same story, is it different? It looks familiar. It's about an aircraft being flown into a building. So far, so good — we think we know where we are with this one. But the details aren't right. This is the other 9/11, that other and rather small-scale vengeful bolt from the blue, the private version you might not have heard of. It's March 2007 and the upturned tail of a light aircraft is sticking out of the smashed weatherboarding of a house in Bedford, Indiana. At first this also appeared to be an accident. Then the police learned of a connection between the pilot and this particular address. It is the home of Vivian Pace, the mother of the pilot's former wife, Beth Johnson. The pilot, Mr Eric Johnson, had had his daughter Emily to stay with him over the weekend, but she had not returned to school when expected on Tuesday morning. Beth had been worried and repeatedly tried to call Eric on his cellphone. Finally he answered but would say only that he had Emily and was going to keep her. They were already in the air, Emily perhaps enjoying this special treat, this extra time with her father. Beth Johnson thought she had a custody dispute on her hands; an abduction, perhaps. She headed for the Bedford Police Department to file a missing person report. By the time she got there Eric had already flown his aircraft into the side of his mother-in-law's house. The meaning of it all became clear when the officers at the scene examined the wreckage of the plane and found two bodies: the pilot and, in the passenger seat at his side, his eight-year-old daughter. It was a parental child-killing for the connoisseur. Where he got the idea from, no one can say.

Understanding these things, I have become uncivilised, unfit for public office – in my case, a side effect of no practical significance. But I wonder if it is a good rule that those who must wrestle with these problems can only be those who do not understand them. In recent history the application of this rule has produced poor results.

*

For the stealer of my children I admit to a tormenting, but entirely proper loathing and when I ask myself if she could ever safely be left alone in a room with me I cannot be sure of the answer. I pore over an imaginary crystal ball, keen to get a clearer prophecy of this awkward but compelling question. Perhaps this will be what game shows are like in their final decadence – the producers select a gladiatorial pair to be locked in the Big Hate House. The audience backs their judgement with cold hard cash and settles down for the show. Our neighbours' domestic incidents have always had a certain entertainment value; surely this would only be one very small extra step. And so, at the end, cued by spasmodic lighting effects and frantic music the door finally opens. Who comes out? Just me? Just her? Tomoko is not to be underestimated. Do we confound everyone and come out chatting and laughing about all that water under the bridge? Perhaps no one comes out and we find hell together in a suitably

Dantesque moment. I would guess that our children's mourning at this 'two birds with one stone' news would be brief – and who would we be to complain about that? I don't know what the outcome would be. How could anyone know?

What about a bit of contrition after the event? Well, I'm not sure about that either. It's expected these days – a verbal ritual to which we make verbal obeisance. But is it honest? There are unforgivable crimes. There are justifiable, or at the very least mitigated murders. The drift of our high moral standards away from the crime of passion has been a drift away from honesty, away from telling the truth about what we really are. It's austere, no doubt, but I'm rather committed to the truth.

*

So much for all that. What of the future, what of better times ahead – if not for those who have caused or suffered irreparable harm, then at least for the next generation once the old, failed one has been packed away? How can the inheritance of hatred be broken? Words may be part of the answer, and though I can't be sure if I will ever meet and speak with my children, or whether this written and admittedly eccentric substitute father will ever find its way to them, there are other words which they have a good chance of finding one day.

I foresee a common scene – one that takes place, appropriately enough, in the sharp freshness of death. There they are, the two brothers, perhaps in early middle age now, changed people my ghost could pass without recognising. Two

Japanese men, each with an unusual first chapter in their life, but one so remote and forgotten that it might almost never have happened at all. Duty has brought them together.

Their elderly mother did not return from her last hospital admission. Her sons were busy, perhaps physically distant and the reports they received too discreet and ambiguous to make the gravity of the situation clear. Each suggested the other should go. Both thought it was just another manipulation, the sort of thing they had wised up to years before. But this time they were wrong, and so when they do finally arrive together there's only a form to sign, and a small bag of personal effects and a set of keys to collect. They go directly to clear the cramped urban flat of her few possessions. They both have to be back at work on Monday.

There's not much at the end of this life — three or four pieces of tired furniture, some foreign books that speak of failed ambitions, an old lady's wardrobe of unfashionable clothes. It can all be boxed up and sent to auction for a few thousand yen. My boys look out the necessary paperwork — bank statements, the last unpaid bills, the rental agreement they must terminate before becoming liable for another month. There isn't much to do. There is small talk and silence.

Makoto looks out at the crowded Osaka cityscape. How is his life going — satisfactory, disappointing, confused? He is at an age to ask more searching questions, to insist at last on uncovering the hidden sources of his self, an explanation as to why it all ended up like this, some more determined backtracking to the point from which it might still have turned out differently. Their mother would never oblige; evasive and theatrically angry, she was skilled at finding ways of punishing them even for asking. The real nature of the game was never admitted, but my boys learned the cost of playing soon enough and gave up. Opposing their mother was a full-time job – better to let it go, to drift into that most essentially Japanese of existences in which everything that most matters is everything that is most unspeakable.

Tomoko worked hard to ensure they were never alone in the apartment for long. Once, it could not be avoided and both boys remember how they talked some courage into each other and ransacked the place in search of a piece of paper – an address, a name, either their father's or the obliterated parts of their own, a photograph, something they could search for on the net. Tomoko, naturally, had thought ahead and none of these things was to be found anywhere – it was never an ordinary home. All they found was an old-fashioned cash box. It was Satomi who was trying to force it open with a knife when his mother came back. They were used to her performances, but this was special the full-throated hysteria, the lurid details of the threatened self-destruction, that old routine that had worked so well for her years before. Then the weeping coda of how it was all their fault, how they had driven her to it. Why were they so cruel? The boys both ran from the apartment swearing they would never come back, though they did – two hours later. Satomi was fourteen, his brother only twelve. The box vanished.

Later, they would hang around the tourist spots to spy on western visitors. They would pick a target and unobtrusively dog him through temple or garden – it would be a man of a certain age, tall, lean, hair neither black nor fair, an approximation to a hazy memory. They would listen in to check that it was English being spoken. If it was crowded it would be an easy matter to brush against a western arm as they checked out his features for a slight resemblance. Over time the sense of a connection dwindled almost to nothing, and then wasn't there at all. And now this — Mother gone too. Makoto feels happy, light, like the man walking from a doctor's surgery having just learned that it isn't cancer, that it really isn't anything at all. The possibility of a less burdened future opens up.

When he turns round he sees his older brother, head and shoulders deep in a futon cabinet as he tugs at something jammed in its lower level. They knew the old girl was a hoarder — they have already dealt with five shoeboxes of department store receipts and stuffed her gold medal collection of three hundred and fifty coat-hangers into rubbish bags. Dusty old shoes come flying out over Satomi's shoulder, a girlish hair clasp with a broken pin. Then he backs out and stands up.

'Remember this?'

There is the lacquered cash box with its damaged lid and, this time, the key tied to its handle with a length of ribbon.

They look through the contents together. There's a protective layer of more or less dull stuff at the top — a forty-year-old foreign ticket for *Death of a Salesman*, another for *The Cherry Orchard*, another for Janáček; strange hints of an earlier life for a woman they never knew to do much more than watch television and clean kitchen utensils to within an inch of their lives. Further down there are photographs of strangers set in a foreign vernacular, no names or dates on the back. A woman who might have been their mother appears in unexplained group portraits of westerners posing against backdrops of institutional grandeur. They study the young men, younger than them by far.

'Which one do you think it is?'

'I don't know. None of them?'

The timeline snakes into the future. There are pictures of children grinning into the icy wind on a Scottish beach.

'Who's that?' asks Makoto.

The round, full face.

'It's you,' says his older brother. 'Do you remember it?'

'No.'

There is a collapsed dragon kite at their feet and no way of knowing now that the distant, formless blur was their mother, the dead woman, jealously sniffing out a moment of happiness, approaching like rain.

Deeper, they find the severed maternity ward wristband, the one I went searching for myself. My sons consider the words 'Galbraith — Boy', briefly speculating on the existence of a secret half-brother before wondering if it might, perhaps, have been one of theirs. Satomi holds it against his wrist — unbelievable. Crisp, folded birth certificates come next, confirming that it is true after all. They use half their names every day, but these documents were hidden because they contained the other half too — it was their blended, cross-cultural wholeness that required them to be locked away. Satomi just about remembers his other names when he sees them. He passes the second certificate to his brother for whom the information is entirely new.

Deeper again through the stack of papers they find more

photographs – smaller, younger selves; Satomi in the garden behind a Reading terrace standing in a pair of unlaced size eleven shoes, Makoto before he could walk, posed on the changing mat studying a copy of the *Complete Works* of William Blake. Their mother appears in some of the images and so the question arises: who is the invisible person behind the camera, the effaced recorder of life that haunts the whole history of do-it-yourself photography? They smile at this person, gesture, run towards him, hold out for his inspection the ladybird crawling up their arm.

There is something else at the bottom of the box, less obviously interesting. It is a packet of letters, rust-spotted where they rubbed against the metal, neatly tied airmails with onionskin sheets inside and foreign stamps on the envelopes from forty years in the past. At first they mean nothing; even the signatory is uncertain – my sons' English, once native, then killed off, has only very partially been revived by their unadventurous Japanese education.

'Here,' says Makoto to his older brother. 'You take them. You must remember more than I do.'

Satomi says he'll give the envelopes to his own son, who might like to soak the stamps off for his collection. But once home he keeps them to himself and stays up late struggling to read the letters his father wrote to his mother before he hated her, or even imagined that such a thing might ever be possible. He works steadily under a lamp and with a translating dictionary at his elbow. It's not easy – these are ancient documents now. It's not only the words that are hard to read, the meaning of the words is hard as well, hard to believe. It's a puzzle, a key. Slowly, nightly, Satomi moves forward. A

cautious, damaged sceptic, he steps across the threshold of the world's only truly sacred place. What emerges from the pages, grasped with a hesitant and doubtful comprehension, is something short of a miracle but which carries with it, all the same, no small healing power.

The whole job takes weeks, but he gets there in the end. He reaches for the telephone and calls his brother.

'No,' he says, 'there's nothing wrong.'

'Yes,' he says, 'I do know what time it is.'

'Well?'

'Listen to this . . .'

8 日本

The modern media-friendly physicist likes to entertain his audience with talk of spacetime, its peculiarities, its fairground tricks that take us to places intriguingly distant from everyday experience. Consider instead not this familiar physical spacetime, but an imagined analogy to help us in our thinking about human affairs: cultural spacetime. It has all the dimensions of its physical cousin but its unit of measurement is the strange rather than the metre or the second. Travellers through its human aether are anthronauts and they measure their journeys in these units of strangeness. The fabric of cultural spacetime is warped just as that of its physical equivalent is said to be, but in a different way. Whereas in physical spacetime a journey into Chinatown is a walk of no more than two or three hundred metres, in cultural spacetime it can equate to a journey of ten thousand conventional miles. Travelling in the temporal dimension has similar, and sometimes dizzying effects. A conversation with an ultra-orthodox rabbi, or a passing sadhu may plunge the explorer of cultural spacetime through a wormhole that transports him back through two or even three thousand units of strangeness to a place where ancient ideas survive untouched by the intervening ages, slumbering in the intellectual mud with all the unevolved simplicity of a crocodile on the banks of the Nile. In cultural spacetime it is not surprising that such a journey into the past should still be disturbed by mobile ringtones or the flickering of departure boards as the partners in this long-distance conversation await their flights. More radically still, the anthronaut, modishly holidaying in the upper Amazon basin or the rainforests of New Guinea can see the clock on his culture-mobile speed down not merely to zero, but deep into negative figures, into prehistory itself, a non-metallic world where a stainless steel teaspoon left behind by a backpacker speaks of other worlds as emphatically as a flying saucer might to you or me if we were to come across it, crashed and smouldering in the local park as we walked the dog first thing in the morning.

Recent work has determined that the shape of cultural spacetime is ultimately spherical – there are limits to the maximum strangeness one can achieve and after a while further travel only brings you home again. So much is plain, but there is one unexpected result. From almost any starting point, when the anthronaut taps 'As Far Away As Possible' into his Cultural Positioning System he finds at the end of his journey that he has always arrived at the same place. Japan.

So what is Japan, the Westerner's archetypal 'other side of the world', to me? Two of its citizens are my children, two of its school pupils, two of the passengers on its trains, two subjects of its laws. I have a stake, and it is larger by far than any I have in the United Kingdom. Wherever my children live must, in part, be my home too. It's a divided consciousness that makes the watch in my mind always nine hours ahead of the one on my wrist. Japan for me is not a subject of study, but a relationship – we're stuck with each other, whether we like it or not. As a relationship it's fascinating, but as dysfunctional as they get. I am Japan's stalker, though such a modest and well-mannered stalker that my quarry doesn't even know I'm there. Its public officials do not accept that I have a stake in their country, nor even a right to know where my children live, or what they look like, let alone to have any say in their future. The only evidence that Japan has of this relationship is the presence of my two children themselves, and it's not evidence that is universally welcomed.

I say I believe my children live there, but for a long time now this has been merely an assumption and if by some dreadful mischance this were no longer true, I doubt anyone would tell me. This makes Japan another wall, or a sinister magical casket into which things vanish and from which they can never be recovered. I am continually uncertain as to whether it is distant at all, or whether it is right beside me. At times I think of Japan as a space just beneath my feet. Like Josef Fritzl's dungeon it's really part of my home, and at the same time stubbornly silent and locked.

*

Should those trained in the strangeness of the United Kingdom have a head start in dealing with the strangeness of Japan? The argument – that suffering from one abnormality gives you insight into another person's different abnormality – is doubtful, but the idea of there being common ground has mileage. Both are islands, nationally and culturally as well as literally. Both base their identity on a delusion about their distinctiveness. In the United Kingdom, particularly to the right of the political centre, it is de rigueur to pretend that one is not living in a European country. In Japan there is a similarly mandatory fantasy about not being part of the dominant continental culture just across the water. The place may be brimful of green tea, chopsticks, seriously good ceramics, pagodas, Buddhist temples and Chinese writing but that is purely coincidental – it's still unique little Japan, not just an East Asian archipelago off the coast of big China. To any suitably distant observer both these ideas are obviously false, mere quirks of national character. They are the intellectual equivalents of bagpipes, or pompoms on a Greek soldier's shoes: identity markers taken very seriously by the natives, but risible to the rest of the world.

Stretching this theme, one could say that both countries had their 1066 moment. A forceful irruption of outsiders that turned everything upside down. In both cases nothing would ever be the same again and the changes would be so finely woven into the fabric of the new identity that the population would come to believe they had always been this way. But that's about as far as the common ground goes; after all, Japan's 1066 did not arrive until 1853. It took the form of the notorious visit of the Black Ships – four vessels of the United States Navy commanded by Commodore Matthew Perry who had been instructed to insist on being received by Japan, and to ensure trading rights for whichever of his countrymen wished to follow. This was an armed courtesy call, the diplomatic equivalent of axing a hole in your host's door and shouting 'Here's Johnny!' through the gap. Nothing new there, I hear you say, and this was indeed one of the most repeated patterns of history since Columbus shipped out in the late fifteenth century. The various European versions of these visits – Spanish, French, Portuguese, Belgian and above all British – tended to turn the host's accommodation into something between a butcher's shop, a slave colony and an opium den. The pre-existing culture was either permanently sidelined or subjected to a lengthy humiliation, typically not thrown off until the middle or latter half of the twentieth century. Japanese anxiety on Commodore Perry's arrival was neither uninformed, nor unreasonable.

More plausibly, the real difference between the two countries lay in Japan's choices over the previous two hundred years – a long, fearful opting out of world history brought to an end only by Perry's visit. For Japan the sea was a moat, for Britain a road which it travelled more widely and to greater effect than any other nation. Even Perry's brusque interruption of Japan's two-hundred-year-long conversation with itself was a part of this Anglo-Saxon expansionism – more Brits really, but updated versions with different accents and different political ideas.

For Britain and Japan to be more similar island nations there would have to have been a Britain that never went travelling. This alternative Britain might have started with the assassination of Francis Drake by a patriot outraged at his having gazed upon a foreign ocean. Once this insult to Englishness had been dealt with, the country would have settled to a long and self-absorbed modesty. Not having seen the world, or brought any part of it home, this alternative Britain's stock of ideas and styles would have remained small and fixed. Instead of finding new things it would content itself with elaborating old ones. In this Britain, the highest expression of culture would be the Beer Ceremony, a highly ritualised manner of downing a pint which would be held to convey the essential nature of the British national character. The nation's limited diet would have resulted in three hundred and eighty-two different ways of preparing wheat, one of which would be the manufacture of wheat paper. Aspiring poets would write on this authentically British material with deliberately unusable implements because ballpoints were for foreigners. They would only write sonnets because that was the tradition and nothing else was allowed. They would be written in a limited vocabulary not much changed since the late Middle Ages and everyone would agree that if there was something for which there wasn't a word, then it was probably a bad thing and one shouldn't be writing about it anyway. In stay-at-home Britain someone did once write an unauthorised villanelle, but they were hunted down and hacked to death by the youth wing of the British National Poetry Society. The Archdruid of Canterbury preached a homily on toleration, explaining how this virtue had its limits and inviting all right-thinking people to join him in respecting the sincerity of the killers, the purity of their motives. As stay-at-home Britain moved timidly into modernity, its television news bulletins would convey the vital results of national daffodil arranging championships and fevered speculation as to who would be appointed to the coveted post of Queen's Morris Dancer. Whenever foreigners derided this stay-at-home culture it would be taken as further proof of its treasured distinctiveness, of outsiders' hopeless inability to understand. This is the fate Britain avoided by travelling, the fate Japan did not avoid by staying at home and giving up the wheel.

After such a long isolation, history suggests that the arrival of the United States Navy should have done to the Japanese what Francisco Pizarro did to Atahualpa. Given that we now live in a world where you can park your Nissan, arrange to meet friends later by texting them on your Toshiba and then head on to the concert where someone with an unpronounceable name does the business on a Yamaha grand piano, it's clear that something very different happened. We are so used to this that we rarely reflect on just how extraordinary it is.

Perry's arrival and the start of Japan's more or less reluctant engagement with the world began a process that, within a hundred and thirty action-packed years, would allow some Americans to make a living writing panicky books about how the Yellow Peril were buying up all the best real estate in New York and Washington. This phase wasn't to last, but that doesn't undermine the fact that the dash from handicrafts to bullet train was a unique event, history's ultimate turnaround. The details are for the scholar; what interests me is that this was not principally a story of industrialisation, but one of preserving a separate identity, of embracing the foreign with the conscious intention of being better able to resist it. The result is a modern country which has never resolved any of these questions, one that has an endless bipolar debate where others have a more settled, confident sense of self. Today's Japanese family in search of entertainment can choose between baseball or sumo, but they cannot do so without some lingering political subtext. In trade, modern Japan's principal medium of communication with the outside world, it is still doubtful whether a sale is meant to bring a customer closer, or to obtain from him the resources to keep him distant. For all the transformations of the last hundred and fifty years, the earlier passion for separateness still defines what it is to be Japanese.

I once came across a trace of this process in a second-hand bookshop in the West End of Glasgow. There was a box full of old scraps – letters, prints from disbound books and a photograph of three rows of serious young men staring hard at the lens. Waistcoats, watch chains, the gowned professor in the middle of the front row, all there to record the local Naval Architecture class of 1895, or thereabouts. The names at the bottom confirmed it – a full third of the class was Japanese. Although at this stage they couldn't possibly have known it, here were the future builders of the aircraft carriers of Pearl Harbor and Midway, of the great *Yamato* battleship whose last futile gesture in April 1945 would end the chapter they were beginning. What on earth were they doing in my home city? It turns out that they were by no means the first. They were following in the footsteps of a fellow by the name of Yozo Yamao, Glasgow's samurai about town thirty years previously. Yamao was one of five young men smuggled out of Nagasaki one dark night in 1863 in breach of the seclusion laws. The plan was that they would learn everything needed to turn Japan into a modern country. Naturally enough, Yamao headed straight for Glasgow where he worked in the shipyards by day and studied for his engineer's certificate by night. While there he fell in with one of the classic types of the age, Henry Dyer, pride of Bellshill, one of the new men who accelerated the world everywhere they went. Dyer went to Japan where he became Professor of Engineering at the

Imperial College at the age of twenty-five thanks, in part, to his friend Yamao. The two men made a sizeable contribution to the modernisation of Japan, Dyer later writing a laudatory book describing the country as the Britain of the East, the highest compliment possible. The photograph left behind in the bookshop was a photograph of their protégés.

The Emperor of Japan appointed Dyer to the Order of the Rising Sun – third class, of course; all that a foreigner was allowed. As for Yozo Yamao, his influence is still to be felt in the lives of modern Japanese at the end of every High School and University graduation when the traditional song *Hotaru no Hikari* is given another lachrymose performance. Apparently it was Yamao who introduced it as part of his educational reforms. The words are Japanese – something about fireflies and ceaseless striving for self-improvement – but the tune is one he would have remembered from his Glasgow days. You and I would recognise it as 'Auld Lang Syne'.

The temporary Glaswegians in the photograph were destined to play their part in Japan's most disastrous wrong turning in its scheme to resist the West by mimicking it. The wealth and the machines they would create would be used to attack, humiliate and exploit Japan's neighbours for thirty-five years until the descendants of Commodore Perry turned up again and stopped them in the summer of 1945. There was more than enough cruelty and arrogance in this episode to justify the harshest criticism, but when I hear the case against Japan being made in a western voice I am still struck by the speaker's lack of self-knowledge. The whole costumed caval-cade of Japan's empire, from the dreadnoughts to the preposterous Ruritanian uniforms, to the statesmen in their claw-hammer coats and silk toppers, the cynicism of their propaganda and the relentless, browbeating indoctrination of the next generation, are all things which the western critic will find so familiar he surely cannot fail to detect his own features in the mirror. Like its industry, Japan's colonial bad behaviour was learned from us.

In 1945 the task was to make another new Japan and this too would be an ambiguous experience – partly a drawing out from its ancient bashfulness, partly a new seclusion under the wing of an American mother hen. Whereas for western countries the process of reconstruction would be about meeting the needs of individuals, in more collectivist Japan it would be another grand national project. The postwar Japanese citizen remained disciplined and undemanding as a consumer. The fruits of his labour were largely exported, his reward an uptick in the quarterly statistics. The results, as before, were quickly impressive and then dramatic. Those out competed by the flood of motorcycles, cameras and radios grumbled ineffectively about war by other means. They were wrong about that. This new Japan's pacifism would prove to be sincere and enduring, and it would soon add another level of uniqueness to the country. Never before had such industrial power accompanied such a restraint of ambition – a genuine historical novelty and a fitting rebuke to the western empires Japan had once imitated.

Of the few remnants of Japan's flirtation with militarism, one is more visible than the rest and can still be seen about the streets of an afternoon when the schools have emptied. The boys appear in Prussian tunics and the girls in sailor suits

— Prussian too in origin, though here recalling the German lust for colonies and for a great navy like the British with which to seize and hold them. These days they are displayed with a thorough innocence of their history. Smile at the wearers, one of my sons perhaps, and they'll respond with the peace sign.

And what of Perry? He got his face on a stamp, several, actually. One other thing — his middle name was Calbraith. Perhaps this was merely an idiosyncrasy on the part of his parents, or perhaps it indicates some ancient clan connection and that I am, therefore, some very remote relative of his. A gene for a fateful fascination with Japan? Probably not worth pursuing.

And the personal in all this politics? It's not hard to see — have a child with a Japanese woman and you have a child with all her problematical history too.

★

I lived in Japan before ever visiting it. After all, countries are really ideas more than they are places. My relationship with Tomoko drifted into this Japan of the mind but it started elsewhere, in a very different cultural and intellectual space, the great non-country where everyone is welcome and equal — portable, unlocated and cosmopolitan, it is still my home though it hasn't been hers for a long time and, I think, never really was. It never has that many Japanese residents, but she seemed to belong there — a high-level student of English literature and all-but-perfect speaker of the language. When questioned about her country of origin she would declare the subject to be just too boring, or confess to what was often a genuine ignorance. There was every sign that hers was a complete and successful escape, away from culture and towards self-determination, the achievement of a deliberate personal project to be free. That's the problem with living in Cosmopolis: it's no one's territory and so those who live there can struggle to understand how very different they are from the nationalised run of humanity.

Territory arrived in a double dose – a house and a child. It arrived with such suddenness that I awoke like a Berliner who never bothered to read the papers, astonished to find a wall across the street and himself on the wrong side. All the more astonishing when one side of the wall is Reading, Berkshire and on the other side it's Japan. Even before my first son was born it already looked bleak. Leave? The damage would have been less and perhaps I would have found a way of living with it, of telling myself it was justifiable. I stayed – and the consequences of this decision were an exhausting six-year rearguard action against the forces of culture and race that ended as it was always going to end. Either I would resort to being a child-abductor, or she would.

Step by step I found myself backing into the position of being a disenfranchised subject of a miniature Japanese colony. Like those who had experienced the real thing in Korea and Manchuria, or in other contexts elsewhere, I found that every treaty was abrogated – first undermined, then actively campaigned against, then openly reneged on before being erased from the record and replaced with an alternative memory so that it had never existed in the first place. I have already described how the names of our children were changed, but this was only one part of an increasingly obsessive programme of cultural aggression. Our children's natural inheritance of bilingualism was a constant battleground and Tomoko worked tirelessly to deprive them of this advantage. My sense of the Japanese language is still tainted by the memory of it being used as an endless, shrill overlay whenever English was used in the home. There would be a telling moment several years down the line when Satomi — the reconsecrated Finlay — was being discussed with the head teacher of his primary school. I was explaining, still with a liberal multiculturalist's misplaced pride, that his Japanese was better than his English and so he might need a little more time to settle in.

'Oh,' she asked. 'And why is that — is it just because he spends more time with Mum?'

'No' was the correct answer, and had we been alone I would happily have gone on to explain that it was because Tomoko always had more batteries in her megaphone than I did. It's how I would see it sometimes, in the toy-littered field of combat — the robots of nationalism always seemed to be tooled up with Duracell, whereas my mild-mannered and pathetically out-gunned opposition had to make do with the equivalent of Tesco's value brand.

For a while I was mystified by the driven quality of this behaviour from Tomoko. Wouldn't any ordinary person get tired of stridently talking over every word of English in their own language hour after hour, day after day? It seemed out of place in the early twenty-first century — more the sort of thing that should have been dressed in old-fashioned khaki with vaudeville jodhpurs, a swagger stick under its arm and a psychotic polish on its boots. I thought of this as a joke the first time it occurred to me, but it turned out to be not so far from the truth. I realised this when I stumbled on a reference to a cartoon that showed a Japanese schoolboy throwing his English textbook into the bin while his mother — who else? — sprinkled salt in the purifying gesture of a Shinto priest. It dated from the early 1940s and stated plainly that English, the language that had been Tomoko's route out of Japan, was the language of the enemy. While Tomoko was, by a good long way, a post-war child she never had the upbringing that should have been hers. Instead, the death of her mother pushed her back a generation into the hands of her grandmother and I came to believe that something must have been done to her in those early years which she could not now remember, or understand, or resist — something that was now forcing her to draw directly on the poisoned wells of the thirties and forties. A parasite of the mind had been planted, one that had lain dormant for decades, just waiting for territory to bring it back to life and action.

In larger, more public conflicts those who would seize control direct their forces to the television station. So it was with Tomoko, though in her case the coup against unacceptable foreign influences in the media involved a single set and a single satellite dish. I came home one day to find a massive machine blotting out one corner of the room and a slim black box underneath it. There was a weather report on, and the map was Japan. She looked immensely pleased with herself and from that point on lived in a media world thousands of miles away from the reality outside the window — and forced our children to do the same.

The war against English culminated in the abduction itself — the head teacher glancing at the fake note and handing over Satomi in a way that would erase her anglophone influence as well as mine. The subsequent telephone calls were the final stage of the process. Over the months, I heard my children's English die and be replaced, word by word, by the winner's language. 'Too far' is one of the last things Satomi says to me in English. Next comes 'wakaranai' — I don't understand. It's what his mother had always been aiming at. It was a narrowing, an unashamedly racist victory over what were once broader and more open minds. It was the circumcision of the tongue.

What with the children's names, the language and the television, the creeping nipponism of the cuisine, the ingeniously worked up hostilities over every negligible cultural norm and the all-consuming fetishisation of shoes, by the time the 747's wheels finally skidded down on Japanese concrete the place was by no means as foreign to me as to the average first-time visitor.

Shoes? Ah yes — here we get to the heart of the matter. In the Middle East they might throw them at each other, but in Japan it's decidedly more odd, and decidedly more important. As an authentic holder of the Japanese identity one could be coldly dismissive of the idea that the Emperor is descended from a sun god, cheerfully un-obsessed with one's blood group, commit oneself to the heresy that cherry blossom of a more or less passable standard can be found beyond one's home shores and even contemplate marrying a foreigner and still, just about, be Japanese. The one thing you cannot be without finally surrendering any meaningful connection with the people of the Rising Sun is relaxed on the subject of shoes. Without an obsessive-compulsive anxiety disorder relating to shoes one can never be truly Japanese. The man who returns from a long company posting abroad and crosses a domestic threshold without giving his footwear a second thought has died as a son of Nippon.

The shoe anxiety is Japan's kosher and halal rolled into one. That is to say, there might once have been some point to it but that was long ago and to introduce rationality into the whole affair these days would be nothing less than an insult. In a society that had not discovered the chair until relatively recently — or the table with legs longer than twelve inches — Japanese life was largely conducted on the floor. Keeping it clean made perfect sense, but one realises this has ascended from being a practicality to a habit, then to a cultural marker and finally to a diagnosable disorder when watching a man walk in his indoor shoes to the edge of one floor surface, then change to plastic flip-flops for the three feet of well-scrubbed stone flagging between that point and the exterior door, then change again into outdoor shoes — and all this in the dry, I might add — and then change once more into a clog like device after he has got into his car so the soles of his outdoor shoes don't touch the ritually unclean pedals. At times, the amount of sheer physical activity in the driver's footwell resembles an organist tackling one of Bach's more demanding compositions.

During visits to Japan I had to watch Tomoko lose her battle with her home country and with the ever-increasing neurotic magnetism of her personal past. It was inevitable that as her confusion reached the acute phase symptoms would take a shoe-related form. In the characteristically minuscule Japanese house we briefly occupied, three sets of shoes would be needed to travel ten feet. In an effort to save on this labour she developed a technique of jumping from one room to another like a hopscotch player or a child dancing around the cracks in the pavement, not because it's fun but because some invisible bully says they have to. When this was no longer enough she was driven to walk everywhere on tiptoe in an attempt to minimise contact with any surface. In the terminal phase locomotion could only be achieved in a sort of frantic, mincing flurry like a performer in a game of charades trying to convey the idea of walking on hot coals. Having lived with similar behaviour back in the United Kingdom, I was unsure just how abnormal it was. Now that I was in Japan would I see everyone else behaving the same way? The intense stares and exchanged glances of concern tipped me off to the fact that she had drifted out beyond the cultural pale. Even in the opinion of her own shoe-juggling relatives she'd finally gone completely nuts.

It is hard to think of another identity as ineluctable as that of Japan. The more third world styles of Roman Catholicism might be comparable, but this is not a race – total escape is rare but it is possible; there is no final genetic barrier. Jewishness, perhaps? At first sight it fits more closely, but under its umbrella there is still such diversity and a relish for loud disputes that it can only be a very limited model. Inside the Japanese identity there is, by contrast, an eerie quiet. If cultural identities were gravity, Japan would be the black hole. It's hardly surprising that Tomoko was first made sick in her attempts to resist it, and then failed altogether.

*

On my first day in the country we are invited to Tomoko's sister's house and it is my turn to be the anxious guest, the first westerner to cross this threshold, just as Tomoko was the first Japanese to be examined in any detail by my own relatives. The hospitality is exemplary and our hosts deal with my hesitancy and my social ineptitude with patience and tact. The gathering is lightened and made easier – for me at least – by the presence of five children: the three daughters of the family and my own two boys. Makoto is the youngest at just less than one year old. Like all one-year-olds he does not do travel, let alone culture shock. His frustration at having to sit still in a plane for eleven hours is all the more understandable because in his mind it never actually goes anywhere – you start off in the world, then sit in a noisy metal room for an eternity only to discover on opening the door that you're still in the world and might as well not have bothered. Granted, the people are slightly different, but then that's true of the people on the other side of the hedge so really, why . . . hold on – what's this? He finds a small plastic Godzilla under the table and settles down to chew contentedly on its tail. Our hosts are aghast at this breach of the hygiene taboo, but I give them no encouragement – it's Makoto and me on one side of the table, culture on the other. I admire his infant insouciance, and need it too. I stick close to both my boys throughout, just like the stereotype of the

Japanese tourist running to keep up with his guide through the blistering psychological assault of a weekend in Paris.

By the standards of contemporary Japan it is a traditional household. This is certainly true in the architectural sense: a single-storey structure, the rooms floored with tatami matting and divided by screens, the whole arranged around a charming courtyard in which a camellia blooms brightly. It is a hundred years old, a great age in wood-built and fire-prone Japan. I am invited to appreciate the original roof beam, still recognisably tree-like with its knots and short stumps where the branches were roughly stripped. Once it was a farmhouse surrounded by rice paddies, now it is part of a dormitory suburb, all but completely deserted because of the long working hours of nearby Osaka. I recognise the setting from the cinema screen, from films made fifty years or more in the past.

Socially, it is traditional too. I say it is Tomoko's sister's house, but that is merely to explain the invitation — it is Tomoko's sister's husband's father's house. Three generations live here, partly expressing a conservative social norm and partly the economic impossibility of acquiring property except through inheritance. Many Japanese lives involve a long wait not to be under someone else's thumb and they are often old themselves before achieving it. Mr Yamada is the patriarch, a genial retired railway inspector who explains that he can never relax on a train journey because he can't stop noticing all the minor defects that tell of a Japan that isn't quite what it used to be. Mrs Yamada arrives later, returning from a long journey to visit a sick friend. She is warm and engaging — as far as the language barrier allows.

Though I learn nothing of their personal history, it seems to me that this is a marriage that might well have begun in the 1940s, or at the latest before anyone waved goodbye to General MacArthur. As such, it as long as the age.

Next in line is Tomoko's brother-in-law, Taisuke, a quality control inspector in a precision engineering company. He is a little shy, much like myself, and can hardly have been looking forward to these social obligations. Fortunately, he is also more linguistically able; his High School English warms up as we go along and makes a major contribution. His wife is my wife's older sister, so here is someone who intrigues me both as a person, and as part of the explanation. I know that Emiko's presence is the result of an arranged marriage and she therefore represents a declining tradition in modern Japan. More than the others, she seems to belong in this hundred-year-old house. Despite being a married woman and mother of three daughters she must accept a low status in the household, and as her children were born to the Yamada name rather than having it conferred upon them it is not even clear that she outranks her own four-year-old.

This expresses itself in a very striking behaviour – Emiko notes my status as an adult male guest by carefully avoiding eye contact with me at all times. Though I have never been in her home before, my arrival has already bumped her down the pecking order. I haven't been forewarned of this and fail to grasp that it is a cultural rather than an individual act. No one else is subject to the same rule, least of all Emiko's three children who feel no need at all to conceal their curiosity. I decide it can only be coyness on her part and make increased efforts. This makes life harder for her and descends, before I finally give up, into a cross-cultural comedy of errors in which I play the increasingly impatient diner and Emiko plays the overworked waitress utterly determined not to see me. There is no literal veil over her eyes; nevertheless, there is something almost Islamic about the scale of the implied unfairness beneath it all. I find this all the more extraordinary precisely because I am married to her sister – a woman for whom the phrase 'in your face' might well have been invented. Indeed, Tomoko's tirades on the subject of my inadequacies often featured the 'look at me' routine: she never had a problem with eye contact. How on earth do these two women share a common background?

Towards the end of the evening meal, when a modest but significant amount of sake has been consumed, Taisuke leans across the table and reveals that he has been pondering the same mystery. He carefully indicates Tomoko with a shift of the eyes, and then glances at his own wife. Leaning in for a better chance of confidentiality, he murmurs –

'Very different. *Very* different.'

Had his English been more colloquial I feel sure he could have spelled it out more clearly. Something along the lines of 'Bloody hell! Rather you than me, mate.'

He is happy with his choice, or rather, with his arrangement. By contrast I already know that I am locked into a situation that is heading for almost certain failure. Through Emiko I understand for the first time the rarity and the scale of Tomoko's great escape. I understand also that it was a tragedy for her, as well as for our children, that she was ultimately unable to sustain it.

The two most important presences at this meal are the

people who aren't there. They stand over and direct the sisters – with, I would guess, an equal influence notwithstanding that one is long dead and the other very much alive. I become aware of them as I watch Emiko and Tomoko and realise that there must be another difference between them which has nothing to do with culture or education. I deduce that Emiko, being several years older, has memories of her mother. She will have a powerful sense of loss, but not the damaging nothingness that is all Tomoko ever finds when she goes to the same place. This can never be more than an amateur diagnosis, but it fits with a persuasive precision as I start to read it into every detail of the contrast between the two women – into Emiko's calm, her evident sanity, into the cast-iron solidity of the Yamada family and the security and confidence of its three youngest members. For Tomoko there is no such solid ground. Her life is one of constant emotional vertigo. She is at sea, and this is why.

I used to think that if I gave enough I could make good this early damage. I had been having doubts about this theory for some time but it was only then, between watching Emiko pour more sake for her husband and reaching with my chopsticks for a confection of fish eggs and seaweed, that I realised I could never have done this, that no one could. Straight away, there came the thought that Tomoko's escape, her apparent revolt against such narrow origins was not individualism at all, but drift. What I had originally read as a woman who knew her own mind was, all the time, nothing more than a woman trying to build a life on loss rather than on more reliable foundations – a loss she would pass on to her children as the closest thing she had to an heirloom. Tomoko's return to

Japan would be as much personal as cultural: a quasi-magical attempt to find her way back to her dead mother by imitating the self-sacrificing rootedness of her sister, the woman who had all the childhood memories she lacked.

The other notable absence was a man I had expected to be there. I had been nervous about meeting him, but hopeful, and it was only a day earlier, probably in an airport, that I learned this meeting would not take place. The explanation was an obvious lie and suggested, rightly as it turned out, that it would never take place. Tomoko's father had no desire to see his grandchildren. On the contrary, he had a very definite desire not to see them or any part of the new, more free and blended world they represent. I had long had the sense that here was an icy and distant character, rarely referred to by Tomoko and never with any affection. But these terms hardly seem adequate to describe a man who will not go ten miles out of his way to meet his grandchildren for the first time. I began to think of both of my boys' maternal grandparents in the same terms – equally damaging, equally dead.

As for the Yamada family, they are good people and although it has been a very much shorter journey for her, Emiko's marriage into their midst begins also to seem like an escape. They might be a good extended family for my children, though I know Tomoko is an outlier in this group, a semi-exile, and what connections there will be outside these formal social occasions is hard to tell. After the abduction I hope there is some regular contact – their stability and ordinariness are just what my boys will need as an asylum from their mother. Whether or not this ever happens, I can't say. Later, they will deny knowledge of my children's whereabouts and refuse to co-operate by passing on any information. The outward forms of hospitality are one thing, but in the end it's still the taking of sides that proves more powerful.

*

Snapshots. Another airport, another time. Marooned in the middle of a vast concourse I am standing alone with Makoto drowsing in the pushchair. From a considerable distance we are spotted by a man in a uniform with a prodigious array of insignia and gold braid. He is obviously very important and is heading our way at a brisk pace. I check for lines on the floor I shouldn't have crossed – these are taken very seriously at Japanese airports. That doesn't appear to be it. Check shoes. No, everyone's wearing them, even the fast-approaching official. I am about to put up my hands and plead for mercy when he walks right by, crouches down by Makoto, breaks into a broad smile, makes a stream of adoring noises, strokes the boy's porcelain cheek, says something congratulatory to me and then marches on. Have I got the place all wrong? The incident is by no means a one-off. We are mobbed by cooing pensioners at a historical site. At a railway station a flock of schoolgirls starts waving from another platform and are so overstimulated by the sight of our mixed-race children that there is nearly a disaster when the train comes in. Later, in a park, a similar band of baby-loving fifth-formers catches us on open ground and surrounds us. *Kawaii, kawaii* they chirrup and at one point need to be physically fended off. Clearly Japan is a child-friendly, multiracial paradise and there's just no pleasing me.

Fast forward a couple of years and there we are again —
same mixed-parents, same mixed race children, only a little
older, a little more specific, more individual, less *kawaii*. This
mysterious K-force in Japanese culture is usually translated
as 'cuteness', but that doesn't convey its full importance. Its
real purpose is to represent, in cuddly cartoon form, that one
has no opinions of one's own, no individuality and no intention of challenging the establishment. It's a squirming,
vacuous giggle accompanied by an upturned glance through
unfeasibly emphasised eyelashes — preferably with a pair of
eyes digitally patched in from a spaniel puppy. All very
winsome, so long as you forget what it means. What it means
is 'please don't hurt me' — and that means that in Japan losing
your cuteness is no joke. On this later visit there are no
fawning geriatrics and not even any packs of schoolgirls prac-
tising their moves for motherhood. They have been replaced
by frigid hotel reception staff who look at us as if we're trying
to book a room in 1950s Mississippi, and a woman on a train
who glares disapprovingly and inches away from Satomi with
open disgust. As soon as my children stopped looking like
toys they had to settle for what they'll always be in Japan:
mixed-race people in a pervasively racist society.

Wind the film forward — another shot. Kyoto this time,
the Florence of the East — or at least it will be as soon as Italian
town planners cover three-quarters of their city in low-cost
concrete gimcrack. I doubt there can be another city in the
world that offers a more dispiriting first appearance to the
traveller. It's not that there aren't hundreds that are worse, it's
the yawning gap between reasonable expectation and reality.
Getting off the train at Kyoto is like one of those slow-motion

scenes in which long-separated lovers run towards each other against a background of pounding surf, only in this version it doesn't end with a kiss but with her booting you in the groin – repeatedly. It would be fatuous to advise the first-time visitor to Kyoto not to despair, but I do recommend some post-despair persistence. The city has another trick to play with your expectations: that it is, astonishingly, well worth the effort after all.

Its great, if well hidden cultural reserves attract both the tourist and the Japanese nationalist fruitcake for whom Kyoto's temples and museums offer a day trip into the past, when a samurai could bisect an insolent artisan with no questions asked, and the wheel was a distant cloud on the horizon. My family play the tourists and come around the corner one hot summer's day slap bang into the other lot. What I first notice is a repainted armoured vehicle, a Casspir, late of the South African police but now blue and with an oddly European double-headed eagle painted in white on the radiator grille. It has come to a halt outside one of the major temples and a young man on top harangues passers-by, his words amplified to an ear splitting volume by the loud speaker vans parked just behind. Tomoko is too embarrassed to translate, but it is easy to guess at his drift, the unvarying staple fare of the Japanese ultra-right – casting doubt on the loyalties of the long-standing Korean minority, magnifying some isolated crime committed by an immigrant worker (one of the few to penetrate Japan's labour market), agitating for the expulsion of American armed forces from Okinawa, picking a fight over an uninhabitable rock in the China Sea, relentlessly hinting at the foreignness of *demokurashii*, the humiliation of submitting to the outsider's system with all its tiresome debate and compromise, damming up the old pure sources of *nihon seishin*, the true and unadulterated spirit of Japan.

The orator's countrymen do not pause to listen. Twenty metres further on an air-conditioned coach debouches a group of tourists, American retirees by their appearance, some of whom — the men at least — may have been here before. They look over towards the commotion but are quickly shepherded into the calm of the great Nishi Honganji temple. In the immediate vicinity of the armoured vehicle only I stand out. The young man shouting into the microphone catches sight of me in the crowd — eight inches taller than everyone else and with politically unacceptable hair I am, unmistakably, the nigger in his personal Asian woodpile, a psychologically charged image that has attracted, repelled and confused his nation for a hundred and fifty years. Worse still, an exhausted, oblivious mixed-race child is sleeping in my arms and another standing by my side. In the mental world of the Japanese nationalist, I am one of those deplorable people who has polluted his nation's purity. For him I am the avatar of the occupation GI or sailor, an unnerving reminder of one of his obsessive themes: the sexual consequences of defeat. Our eyes meet and a staring contest ensues until he looks away and continues with his shouting.

I know his history better than he does himself, the parts out of which he is made and how they have come together to make this bombastic, stagey extra straight from the thirties. I also know that in his dream Japan my *haafu* children would be denied employment without explanation, or the benefit of the doubt if they were ever unlucky enough to be accused of a crime. Their careers in the civil service or in industry would never quite take off, however good they were or hard they worked. Provincial guesthouses would often be full to them, though not to the next traveller. At night, in the wrong parts of town, they would be just a little less safe than other people and the police, without one ever quite being able to put one's finger on the reason, would be less interested in finding out what happened.

Later, a jovial taxi driver plies the boys with sweets and chats with Tomoko. The rightists have moved on to block a side road and are lecturing the trapped drivers, who honk back with their horns like frustrated geese. I catch a word of our driver's commentary as we pass by – *chijin*. Tomoko helps with the details.

'Look at these idiots – d'you see what they're doing? And the police – why are they so useless?'

There are plenty of them, both in patrol cars and on foot, watching, milling, waiting for an idea or an instruction. I ask our man why they don't do anything and he is delighted by the question.

'Why? Do you even need to ask? Because they're frightened of them, that's why they don't do anything.'

He shakes his head and speeds up. I look back through the rear window. There aren't really any brownshirts there, but you could see them if you tried.

Another shot – winter this time. It's a few days before Christmas, late afternoon twilight with the odd flake of snow in the air and the temperature falling fast. I am on a long semi-aimless wander around the stubbly rice paddies and scattered buildings that surround Tawaramoto. I head towards the main road and the area's only sizeable super-market in the hope of tracking down a bottle of wine in the 'ethnic specialties' section of their booze department. A worker returning home clears his throat and spits into a drainage ditch with theatrical hostility just as I pass. Half a mile further on a police patrol car appears and slows to walking pace. It kerb crawls me through the gloom for thirty metres, the uniformed occupants peering up through its windows before it surges on, having made its point.

Japan's concerns about cultural purity tend to weaken in the face of a sales opportunity and this means that the coun-try's retailers have enthusiastically embraced Christmas. I enter the supermarket by passing between a pair of illumin-ated inflatable Santas. Bing Crosby alternates with 'Jingle Bells' in an endless loop over the public address system. In an obscure corner I find a couple of bottles of Australian red, both with a fair amount of dust on their shoulders and totally unreasonable price tags. I pick one up anyway, hoping that a little of the grape rather than the grain will assuage my homesickness. The fish counter distracts me – out of curi-osity, not appetite. Oysters languidly gape and squirt the occasional jet of brine, crabs flex their claws; two are engaged in slow-motion combat in a tragic misapprehension of who their real enemy is. Fish gasp, octopus flail, a tub of bootlaces writhe in their own oily slime. The whale steak is one of the few things not still moving. I survey all this in deepening melancholy when an eighteen-inch plastic Christmas tree also stirs into life. First it lights up, then gives itself a bit of a shake. Having gained my attention it opens a wide, crimson gash in the middle of its branches and begins to perform. The familiar German carol sounds out in thin, synthetic tones. It sings at me – 'The people's flag is deepest red, It shrouded oft our martyred dead, And ere their limbs grew stiff and cold, Their hearts' blood dyed its every fold.'

When it comes to Japan, the rest of the world and incomprehension – it's mutual.

The airport again – flying back this time. Satomi is coming down with a cold that gets worse with every passing hour. His patience with this long imprisonment is heroic; there's more risk of a tantrum from me than from him. Makoto is one year old precisely. He joins the mile high birthday club and is presented with an inflatable jumbo jet inscribed in marker pen by the cabin staff. I will find it later, flat and wrinkled at the back of a drawer. I carefully lift it out and add it to the reliquary of my private religion. We are anthronauts for real this time, crossing the cultural spacetime that separates Japan from the rest of the world as well as the more conventional miles. Its strangeness is never more startling than when compressed to a single day's travel.

We depart from Kansai International. Like much of the newer Japanese infrastructure – the poorly frequented toll roads, the pointlessly concreted riverbanks, the elevated motorways that peter out halfway across valleys as if bombed in a silent war no one has noticed – its principal *raison d'être* is to allow for the expenditure of public capital in a largely failed twenty-year experiment in stimulating the economy. And spend they did. At times this vast, gleaming indulgence can be as deserted as a post-apocalyptic film set. It's busier on this occasion, but there is still something unconvincing

about it, especially for a place that calls itself international.
My children are the most international thing there. After
them there's just me and a solitary, mysterious East African
with a hunted look on his face. We jar to a halt as we
encounter each other. There's an instant of eye contact that
says 'Yeah – you and me, friend. You and me', before he
hurries on. We have just had a postmodern, globalised Dr
Livingstone moment and it could only have happened in an
'international' Japanese airport.

The rest of the humanity has clearly all come from a
single supplier – there is a house style, a strictly limited
product range. The ear reveals more variety than the eye –
some Chinese, some Korean. But if it's variety you're looking
for, this is the bonsai version – as big as it ever gets in Japan.
The boarding call for the Seoul flight causes a sizeable exodus.
Oddly, when they're gone I feel even more unnerved.

Again we sit in the metal room. The pilot dials the
co-ordinates, pulls the levers. Many hours later the machine
falls quiet. *Oshimai*, says Satomi; in this context it's something
between 'finished' and 'I can't bear it any longer'. The door
opens. It's still the airport, but how magically transformed.
The world bustles in the arrivals hall – every possible shade
of skin colour and variation of facial features. The staff are as
diverse as their customers. No doubt polyglot to start with,
they have acquired an astonishing range of linguistic skills in
the simple matter of telling people where to queue. I listen in
to a small and highly dynamic south Asian woman with a
badge and a high visibility waistcoat as she deploys, in short
order, a couple of Indian languages, two or three European
and even a few words of Chinese. I am entering a slightly

psychedelic state as she catches sight of us and I half expect
her to address us in Japanese. I bet she can. There is a line that
consists of several white people, a Rastafarian and his friend,
a family of conspicuously attired Orthodox Jews, a loud and
numerous contingent of Cypriots, the aforementioned
Chinese who — by the sound of an argument developing
between their children — are on their way back to Newcastle,
and then us. It's the British Passport Holders' queue. My two
boys blend right in — so far as anyone does. Tomoko is miserable, appalled. As for me, I almost weep with relief at being
home. Here it is: the great non-country, the only one I would
ever fight for. In our contrasting reactions anyone with eyes
to see could have foretold our future.

*

Do I like Japan? I have good reasons not to, but they are
largely personal and in the matter of criticism, as in so many
other areas of life, it makes sense not to mix business with
displeasure. There are many countries I would prefer my
children not to be abducted to rather than Japan — more than
a hundred, I should think. But there are some I would prefer,
including the one from which they were taken: the country
in all the world that is most diffident about its own identity,
the country that would have presented the least risk of them
being excluded or discriminated against.

It would be too much to say that my views on Japan are
those of a disappointed patriot, made harsh only by his keen-
ness to see an improvement in his own country. Japan will
never be that, would never allow it. But there can never be a

complete separation either – because of the woman I was once married to, and because of my children, I have become hyphenated. When I watch a scientist at the British Geological Survey in Edinburgh point to the spikes on his graph and say that this is what the great Japanese earthquake of March 2011 looks like from Scotland, it comes as no surprise to me that I should be able to feel such things through the soles of my feet.

It is easy to make claims of this sort, and on the subject of ourselves and our feelings we are notoriously unreliable. We all need some more trustworthy route to self-knowledge – litmus, touchstone, acid test or what you will. In each case it must have the capacity to take us by surprise and impress itself upon us before more conscious thoughts intrude and lie. For me it is words. Not sentences – I don't trust them at all, but single words and especially those that come unbidden. And so I remember when I was walking back one night, a week or two after midsummer, and it was hot and dark and there had been rain in the last hour and a heavy vapour was rising from the asphalt. Snails were partying on the path, so many that I had to pick my way carefully through them. I crouched down to get a closer look at one big fellow. I tapped him on the shell, as I have always had to do since childhood, just to see him draw in his horns. I looked at him and named what I saw – *katatsumuri. Den den mushi mushi katatsumuri.*

In years to come, after the stroke, I will baffle the speech therapist as she works her way through the flashcards.

'What's this?'

'Scissors.'

'Good. And this?'

'A hat.'

'Excellent. And this one?'

'Katatsumuri.'

'Try again.'

'Actually, my dear — for me, it is. It's a long story.'

It's a shibboleth. You'll know what it means if you're one of my people.

*

A real snapshot to end with. Of the scraps left behind when Tomoko abducted our children to Japan only a single item has much interest for me. It is a collection of photographs dating, from their appearance, from the early 1940s to the mid or perhaps later 1950s. Tracing them back in time I move from a swaddled infant — my former wife perhaps, or the more fortunate first child, her older sister? — through pictures of a journey across water, an economical honeymoon it seems, with a picture of a distant American aircraft carrier as a reminder of other things. And then the wedding photographs, eerily western with the bride in white and the groom poker-faced in hired tail coat and wing collar. I notice that in the other pictures, too, this man never smiles. Further back, freer and happier images: the girls before marriage, dressed exactly like their western contemporaries in ankle skirts and bobbysox, four of them posing together by a prized scooter, characters in an Ozu film, the as yet undisappointed young of MacArthur's miraculously recovering Japan. Then the school years, a succession of group portraits of girls getting smaller and smaller, though always in the same neat sailor

suit uniforms. At the beginning of the series, at the age of nine or ten, the girls of the Elementary School class go on a field trip and are ranked tightly together so the photographer can fit them all in as they stand on a bridge against a backdrop of trees and waterfall.

I try to follow the bride's face back through time and find her as a child under the waterfall. The trail is clear for a while, then uncertain. At the end I am only guessing. All I can say is that one of these girls, the one who would die so young after the birth of her second child, my future wife, was my sons' grandmother.

The more I look at the picture, the more I come to like it. Just as you would expect with an old family photo.

9 *Flood*

We are land animals. When we struggle to explain the worst that can befall us our nature compels us to talk of water. We are overwhelmed, we drown, our hopes are sunk, the waters close over our heads and the heads of those we loved as if they had never been, we founder, we are wrecked. Tsunamis of metaphor and reality surge from nowhere and destroy all that we have built and care for. When the waters recede from a world we can no longer recognise only the unlucky have survived to count their losses. What comes after such annihilations? Is any recovery possible or are we fools to press on when the game is lost, dupes of the self-help parasites, of the bereavement counsellor's cheerful egoism? It is an essential question, for much of life is loss and much of that is irrecoverable. If our literatures and our religions tiresomely harp on the theme of restoration it is only to confirm that in reality these things are impossible — we shall not meet by and by in the evergreen meadows of a second life; Lassie, that matted patch of tan and white hair on the motorway, is not coming home.

We are greatly offended by the idea that loss is absolute and insist on struggling against this obvious fact, sometimes with grotesque results. Out of thoughtless well-meaning and a cringing obedience to received ideas we can barely refrain from congratulating a man on his heightened appreciation of birdsong on the occasion of his going blind. Quadriplegia is a chance to get some thinking done: 'Chin up, handsome

— could be worse.' The afflicted collaborate in the whole strange performance — a double amputee victim of a terrorist bombing discourses on her good luck. Readers may have their doubts, but if any questions are to be raised we would all much prefer not to be the one to raise them first. The journalist assigned to a catastrophe story is a schmaltz-seeking missile heading straight for the miracle rescue and the heartening tale of a community brought together by adversity. If he can find something involving the faithfulness of a dog, so much the better. In the crooked pan-balance of modern tragedy a featherweight of goodness always tips the scales, whatever is on the other side. Something has gone wrong with our weights and measures. We are cheating. The result is like being trapped in a permanent production of Nahum Tate's version of *King Lear* — three hours of total bloody disaster before a fairy comes on and organises a dance routine. Thank heavens for that, we all agree on departing the theatre; some good came of it after all.

Beyond sex and religion there may be no subject on which we are more persistently stupid and dishonest than loss. We know that much of what we say when confronted with these tests is foolish or regrettable, but we find no good alternative and lack the courage for silence. The reason seems to be that we recognise loss as a down payment on death — one of those *sans* thingies on our *sans* this, *sans* that journey towards *sans* everything. Though I would say that Shakespeare chose poorly when he suggested that it was chiefly through the loss of our faculties that we approach death — it is through the loss of other people. Even a dimmed perception of those we love most is a bright piece of life.

And so if loss is a particle of death, the frailty of our thinking on the subject most likely expresses our fear of death, which is in turn not truly an emotion, but merely an evolved behaviour under the lash of the survival instinct, nature's cruellest dictate. Whatever our philosophies, we show a strong tendency to be bitter-enders when it comes to stringing out our own existence. Media announcements of the latest marginal extension to average life expectancy are always positive in tone. Only the actuary is allowed to be reflective – fretting over the cost of it all, insofar as his profession has the right tools to measure it. This will change, and in the not too distant future.

Death and loss differ in one essential respect: loss adds to our burdens while death relieves us of them entirely. Keeping that in mind, the scale of our confusion on the subject is clearest in another context where the panacea of death is said to be the ultimate punishment – surely a strong contender for the world's most blatantly erroneous idea. Death is an early release scheme, a pardon from consciousness that no one who was both punitive and lucid would ever willingly grant. Loss is a superior punishment in every respect, and here the punisher must keep his subject alive as assiduously as the doctor. Loss is the death we wake to, the heart sinking every morning as soon as the mind has sufficiently cleared to know itself. Loss is the one to worry about – and how could it be anything other than cruel to tell the truth about this?

If lying about these things is therapeutic then there might be a case for it as persuasive as that for any other placebo treatment – as long as someone, somewhere knows there's nothing really there, that it's just a sugar pill. Failing that, the risk is too great that all we end up with is an endlessly confused homeopathy of self-help pedlars and grief consultants where even the shamans dispensing the stuff have no idea what they're about and no chance of leading anyone out of the maze. As for me, I prefer the pain – there's something reassuring about its message that a part of me is still working as it should.

*

It is December 2004. I approach a second childless Christmas, although this one will be memorable for other reasons. I check the last posting times for Japan. Wrapping gifts in emotionally upbeat paper suddenly floors me. I have to take a break, to wander the freezing shores. Later, in the seasonally extended post office queue, I wait to make my gesture, my observance and wonder how many others there are sending to addresses that might not be the right one, to people who might not be there. I enclose a note to Tomoko suggesting that, should she feel the need, she could always cut the name tags off the presents and replace them with her own – better than throwing them away. My boys are still young enough not to question the English packaging within. She could always lie about it, maybe next year too. After that, it won't be so easy.

Christmas Day leaves no trace on my memory; probably not on yours either. It's the next day that bites and gives its name to the Boxing Day or the Asian or the Indian Ocean tsunami. It's the first of its kind in the television age and so novelty blends with horror and an intense curiosity. Before

this we don't really know what the word means. I am
mesmerised by the dark hill of water surging towards the
tourist cameras. The rolling news services repeat it endlessly;
a hundred times, two hundred? Not since the start of the last
war have the picture editors been so spoiled. Sunbathers turn
and run across wide expanses of sand – it seems impossible
they can cross it in time. Others are running towards the
wave, towards whichever child or lover is closer to the danger.
Did they hope to save both, or was their preference to save
neither?

In other images the water surges across coastal roads and
inundates the swimming pools of beachfront hotels and then
the lower floors of the buildings themselves. Plate glass shat-
ters under the weight, causing great whale-spouts of air to
shoot up from what is now the bottom of a shallow sea. In the
Magic Lagoon and Resort Spa the bodies of two hundred
guests are recovered from their rooms. A survivor, inter-
viewed later in an airport, recalls a car floating through the
lobby and seeing children separated from their parents by
the force of the swirling waters. Like countless others, the
best he can do is to borrow from mythology. 'It was Hell,'
he says, though the term hardly seems adequate. The profes-
sionals also struggle with their language – all heavy objects
moved by the tsunami are toys. Sometimes toys in a bathtub,
sometimes toys thrown about by an enraged giant, but always
toys of one sort or another. Broken timber can be either
matchsticks or kindling. Once these metaphors are exhausted
there is nothing left but a 'scene of devastation'.

Anyone might struggle to convey such realities and for all
the resources of the modern media understanding comes

slowly, just as it does for the individual thrown instantane-
ously into a new world. The first estimate of the death toll is
twelve or thirteen thousand. Within days this is raised by
degrees to sixty thousand, yet this is still only a fraction of the
truth. One early problem is that the distribution of digital
cameras maps the distribution of western tourists. For too
long it is a story of Swedes and Germans swept from the
beaches of Phuket or crammed into airports as they stam-
pede for the exits. 'Tourist nightmare,' says one story: 'I lost
my mobile *and* my iPod.' Then it eddies out across a widening
list of countries – Indonesia, Thailand, Malaysia, India, Sri
Lanka. It takes a few days, but gradually we come to realise
that most of this happened where no one could afford to
record it.

Hands are an early theme. Three days in, there is a photograph of a father holding the hand of his dead eight-year-old
son. Mostly, it is living hands pulled from each other in the
last moment of contact. Udashika, two years old, is torn from
her mother's grasp in Sri Lanka. On the Indian coast south of
Madras, Raja talks of Anousha, his daughter, to a journalist:
'I had her hand in mine as we ran from the water, but the
wave took her from me.' They will dream of this last touch
as long as they live. They will reproach themselves for not
having the strength to fight a tidal wave. A British mother
tells of how she could only hold on to one of her two children. She lets the older and stronger go and does what she
can to save the younger. On this occasion all three survive.

Even for this exceptional event, the template of disaster
reporting is strictly observed, the stories moving quickly into
the palliative mode. A mother in Penang is certain she has

lost her week-old infant but finds her later floating on a mattress, unharmed and untroubled. Two-year-old Hannes Bergstroem is found by the side of the road and cannot say his own name. The staff at the Phuket International Hospital are unsure of his language and a photograph of a fair-haired boy is posted on the internet. He is recognised in Sweden almost at once and his uncle heads straight for the airport. 'This is,' he says with wearying inevitability, 'a miracle – the biggest thing that could happen.' And yet, when news of Hannes first spread the hospital had to deal with many bereaved Scandinavian parents, all hoping that Hannes would turn out to be someone else. The Bergstroem joy is the joy of the lottery winner – to accept it with complete innocence one must shut out all the rest of the world.

The remaining tropes are given an outing, though not always in the most conventional form. The tsunami really is good news for some people, undermining the walls of an Indonesian prison and bringing an unlooked for clemency to its two hundred inmates who leg it into the anonymous chaos. There is even an outbreak of harmony in the very last place one would look for it – Rabbi Shlomo Amar, Azizan Abdul Razak and the Presbyterian Reverend John Macleod all agreeing that the disaster was a divine punishment for those who had neglected their grovelling duties, or been caught pleasure-seeking on the Sabbath. And one might imagine that nothing less than a tsunami would bring Shlomo, Abdul and Presbyter John together in a common understanding of humanity. Then there is the 'life goes on' routine, and how it does. Some cities piously cancel their New Year fireworks, but London contents itself with toning them down. In the Tiger discotheque on Patong beach there is a candlelit vigil only metres from where the wave crashed in, but the party warms up as the night moves on. In the debit column too, life carries on precisely as before, the private floods not letting up for a moment. Jill Bennett comes home to find her family has also come to an end, but this is Orpington, Kent. Mr Bennett, a forty-one-year-old quantity surveyor, has strangled their daughter and then killed himself. The bodies are found in a setting of Christmas decorations. Meanwhile, elections are looming in the Maldives and the opposition is blaming the government for its seismic incompetence.

All in all, it is a story of loss, but because it is our obsession and the heart of our bad conscience, it becomes a story of children too — how we lose them, how we struggle to find them again, how we fight over them and mistreat them precisely because they are what matters most. The media focus on the loss of children because this approximates to the loss of everything. It is the one detail that just about makes the whole understandable. Conversely, it is the finding of the lost child that gives fullest meaning to the 'miracle' of journalistic cliché. Many children are orphaned or displaced. The youngest are blank, available. Several become the subject of competing claims and in a world where witnesses and papers have also been swept away there is no easy way of deciding between equally passionate demands. There is the awkward, if largely unspoken question of how much this matters. If a bereaved and loving parent steals away a child to a good home this might change the distribution of loss, but not necessarily the quantity. These anxieties take on a more definite form as a story starts to run about child traffickers exploiting the situation. There is a confused account of the motives – they may be sexual, or the aim may be to fulfil the dreams of wealthy would-be parents in the West. There are rumours, unconfirmed reports, talk of a text message advertising three hundred Indonesian 'orphans' for sale, though no one has seen it for themselves, let alone this large stock of goods. In one television piece the cameras wait while a bus transporting children from one of the worst affected areas is searched by officials. We are poised for revelations, for drama. In the event, nothing is amiss. The story staggers on for a few days, then thins out, then disappears altogether. We are relieved, but also a little deflated. The tidal wave becomes less understandable as a result – we could have made more sense of it as a child-stealer.

*

I sit in Satomi's bedroom, as I still call it. It has a dry, slightly dusty smell to it, the scent of not being lived in. The calendar he made at school still hangs on the wall, forever frozen at July 2003. The electric clock has outlasted all my expectations and is only now coming to the end – the second hand can no longer climb the hill and breathlessly fibrillates just short of a quarter to. I consider the child-sized bed, the one whose dismantled parts I will later throw in a recycling skip before handing in the keys to the estate agent.

Unable to shake the images of disaster from my mind, I find a question both personal and general: when to take an axe to this timber? When to make a fire of it, or the posts of a new shelter, or a shrine to what is no longer there? When, or whether, to build a new target for the flood?

Naturally, there is another course and I am keenly aware of it: don't discard the bed, but replace the child and fill it up again with new life. I make a half-hearted note to self — get someone pregnant, rustle up a new purpose in nine months flat, a new voice to cry for me in the night. The eroticism of catastrophe should come as no surprise. No surprise either if the much-vaunted courage to rebuild should be nothing more than a hormonal invisible hand driving us to replace lost stock. If all the evidence of the recent Japanese tsunami were erased demographers could still infer an event of some sort. It would not be long before it became visible — a bump on the fertility graph traceable all the way back to cautious movement under blankets on the High School basketball court amidst the snores of a hundred other evacuees. Catastrophe is nature's Viagra and it doesn't like to be kept waiting. No doubt many of the older baby boomers were conceived before the formal cessation of hostilities in 1945. A good few will owe their existence to the romance of the bomb shelter and the underground station, the blackout knee-trembler. Earlier, there was no drama to the rhythm of loss and replacement, just a steady familiarity. A glance at the headstones of a Victorian cemetery reminds us of the erectile qualities of mortality and just how determinedly they had to keep on plugging away to get two or three through to adulthood. On some stones the dates have a callous order and we are drawn to the suspicion that no choices were being made here, no freedom exercised as they shuttled busily from bedroom to graveside and back.

Replacement does repair loss; never entirely, but more than the individualist would care to admit. One lover replaces another, and in time even one child can replace another. But the central problem of life is that these replacements also recruit for the next disaster. In the stable, prosperous world – seismically as well as politically stable – the odds that we'll get away with it are good. We have a reasoned optimism that we'll die first, reaching the exit before tragedy strikes. As far as the peace of death goes it's very much 'me first' rather than 'after you'. We might behave frightfully well in the queue for the lifeboats, but when it's extinction on offer no one wants to be last. A survivor of the Asian tsunami, a girl who has lost a sibling, explains that she hopes to die before her parents because she cannot bear to see them so grief-stricken again. It's a sort of psychological proof that we really do prefer death to loss and, in addition, a reminder that our appetite for non-existence can be thoroughly selfish.

A parent's enthusiasm for procreation harbours a similar selfishness – we know that in the ordinary course of events we will have the best of our children but will not have to stick around to witness the worst. One of modern medicine's greatest disservices to humanity is that when we die at a technically assisted one hundred years of age we will have lived not only to see our children wither, but our grandchildren enter the disappointments and decline of middle age. When we are young we yearn for the strength of gods to protect our children from all possible harm. As for what happens later, when the tests will be more severe, we can do nothing but console ourselves with the thought that we will long since have resigned our responsibilities. Whatever their

troubles, we shall be home and dry. Through it all we know
that the only fail-safe protection we could have offered would
have been not to bring them into existence in the first place.

This is no school philosophy, but an urgently practical
issue. What if, in some imagined far future, when the wave
rolls in again, there is no one in its way, not even to report its
uneventful passage? Would that not be better, the natural
non disaster? But we will not follow this argument, we will
not have its implications – not at any price.

Warily, I turn back to the empty bed and the clock's
twitching second hand. I think of the collared doves that nest
under the eaves and their mindless persistence in the face of
reproductive bad luck. They will come again in 2005 – it will
be one of their better years, though I don't suppose they
could have known that. As for me – do I want it even to be
possible to lose another child? No decision comes, or rather I
decide both ways, finding two contradictory views of life
equally persuasive. I get stuck between them and this immo-
bilising doubt proves to be a highly effective contraceptive. I
take no further action on my 'note to self'.

*

When the Asian tsunami struck it was one year to the day
since the Bam earthquake in southern Iran killed thirty
thousand people, less a handful or two. The papers had
prepared their anniversary pieces in anticipation of a meagre
newsflow through Christmas and New Year. Those that had
been scheduled early still ran, but the rest were spiked in
favour of the new sensation. This in turn ran as the main

story for only a few days before gradually giving way to a space probe landing on Titan and renewed violence in Iraq in the run-up to its elections planned for the end of the month. A few years later, Japan's disaster gets bumped off the front pages by the death of Elizabeth Taylor. I myself rank high in the list of distracted and egotistical observers. I lose two days' work and then remonstrate with the television screen, explaining how it couldn't have come at a worse time: the last and long-planned chapter of a book involves one tsunami and then another comes along and messes everything up. What are the chances of such improbable collateral damage? Will I have to rewrite the whole thing? I watch a solitary figure clambering over a featureless plain of debris. I feel sure that I know what he is looking for and this is confirmed when a journalist and a cameraman move forward to intrude upon him. He is looking for a photograph, for a photograph above all things. I decide that I don't have to rewrite a word, that this isn't even news.

One of the challenges for the surviving flood victim is to understand how his experience pushes him into a new frame of reference while the rest of the world progresses as if nothing had happened. If this is to be accepted without it becoming an additional injury he must try to understand that while loss, in sufficiently skilled hands, can be the stuff of tragedy, losers are ten a penny and their stories rarely have any particular call on the attention of a listener. The truth is we crew different ships: one man on the *Pequod*, one on the *Rachel*, neither much to blame for their mutual lack of interest. They come together in art, late on in *Moby Dick* when the story is almost done. In all the men of the two ships

Captain Ahab is the smallest, with room inside only for the white whale and nothing else. While pursuing it he is waylaid by the *Rachel,* which steals the wind from his sails and forces him to stop. 'Bad news,' says the old Manxman. 'She brings bad news.' Ahab asks first about the white whale, but the new captain has a question of his own. He is searching for something too — a whaleboat adrift. The two men talk past each other, but the captain of the *Rachel* is insistent, desperate. He demands that Ahab help search for the missing whaleboat, that he put this boat before the whale that obsesses him. He offers him money. Curious seamen look on and one wagers to another that someone in this missing boat must have made off with the Captain's best coat, or even with his watch, such is the man's anxiety to find it.

'My boy,' says the captain of the *Rachel*, 'my own boy is among them. For God's sake — I beg, I conjure . . .'

Ahab refuses. He is losing time and can think only of the whale. He rejects every appeal and sets sail after Moby Dick, damned from this moment on whether he finds him or not. Captain Gardiner goes his own way, weaving wide across the ocean still in the hope of finding his lost child. In the end, the devious-cruising *Rachel* does save a life — not the boy, but Ishmael, the last survivor of the *Pequod*.

For literal losses, even in the absence of a body, there is always a point when it is no longer reasonable to hope. The relief of despair comes at last and a forward step is possible, however halting and damaged. Those left behind by parental abductions have a rarer and more difficult situation on their hands, though it is one the more conventionally bereaved might prefer. The pseudo-death of the parentally abducted child is built up, day by day. Each day is a new unit of loss, a further dilution of whatever connection is left, the passing of one more irretrievable parcel of time. None of this is necessary – it could be discontinued by the abducting parent, but rarely is. And so there is a painful additional element: the awareness of being constantly subject to another's control. Each new day of silence is one the abductor has decided shall be silent. In this prison all the sentences are indefinite and there are no visiting hours. The last telephone has long since been torn from the wall.

Technology has added a new piquancy to this experience. Its most recent manifestation appeared outside my home a couple of years ago – a car which carefully nosed around every corner of the streets with an unfamiliar device on its roof. It captured an image of my own car, the red one I had looked out for at the railway station in the summer of 2003. It captured me also, a gangling blurred upright in another shot that only I could recognise. About the same time Google's Street View cameras wandered the streets of Higashi Toyonaka, past the woman with the red shopping bag, past the vending machines and the local store and the neat allotments on the left, past the Hair Cozy salon and the woman cycling down the other side of the street with her child in the handlebar basket. Past the apartment block where my children live, one camera looking up at the balcony. There is a carousel for drying clothes. Digitally, I tour the neighbourhood hoping to get lucky. There are a dozen or so pedestrians, but as in the dreams, their faces are obscured. The best candidate is a cloud dismounting from a child's yellow bicycle outside what appears to be a nursery. According to the anxieties of the age, he has been effaced with particular thoroughness. These new technologies have the potential to make contact easier and of higher quality. They undermine the excuses for cruelty, but often make little difference in practice. To the abductor mentality they are not relevant. In the autistic world of the family courts they represent a new threat — one recent judicial comment suggested that a father acquiesce in the termination of his family life because he could communicate with his children in Australia over the internet. Telecommunications tantalise the excluded parent but do nothing to improve human nature.

The oddness of this life derives from the fact that no one has really died and therefore the prospect of a future encounter — for others a theological conviction or a private fantasy — remains real. The door might swing open one day and the two realities, divided by the abduction, come back together. This possibility obsesses the left-behind parent no less than the promises of his religion obsess the believer. In both cases the idea is the subject of much anxiety and doubt, as well as hope. In both cases, a portion of this hope, at the very least, is unreasonable. There may be no restoration at all. If the moment ever does come it will not involve the lost child, but an adult shockingly changed from the person one remembers. A stranger will stand there, all the lost years made flesh. And when they first open their mouth to speak it will be impossible to suppress the fear that what comes out will not be their own voice, but that of the abductor — painful evidence of that universal version of the Stockholm syndrome that forms the ambiguous core of every parent–child relationship. One fears that the moment of restoration

will be identical with the abductor's consummate victory.
These encounters cannot all go well and some will be so
painful that they will be regretted by one, or both parties. So
far from being a restoration, they may be a further loss.
Needless to say, I have no such concerns for myself.

*

A supermarket a few days after Christmas, a few days after
the great wave. It's one of those big ones out of town – how
many tills do they have now, fifteen, thirty in a single store?
Such order and repetition produces a powerful perspective,
veering away to a vanishing point just beyond the distant
news-stand and the franchised café. The effect is an ancient
one, sought by the architects of power and mystery from the
Acropolis onwards and repeated endlessly in the Gothic
nave, the baroque colonnade or more grandly in the boule-
vard or avenue terminating in a far-off monument. Here, in
a charmless Scottish supermarket, it survives in a degraded
form, an accidental architecture like that found in the
arrangement of looms in a Manchester cotton mill, or of
desks in a general office typing pool. It still catches me as I
raise my head and am drawn into the image's history and all
its implications. Perspective is about what lies beyond what
we can see – about the fact that what appears to us to be the
vanishing point is always subjective.

I have acquired dangerous habits in these places, especially
for a member of the dangerous gender. I practise brief,
amateurish acts of surveillance, selecting a family or parent
and child and then feigning an interest in nearby yoghurt or

frozen fish or kitchen cleaning products. In more cosmopolitan areas they might, on rare occasions, be Japanese and I like
to listen to them talk. But what interests me more are the
little groups who have chosen neither to be one thing nor
another, the glimpses of the future. The mixture might be
national — a Polish parent and children who chatter with
dazzling facility in sentences that change language halfway
through. I notice that the parent speaks only in their native
tongue, but the children are already free and away —
Europeans of a breed only now coming into existence. There
are bolder mixtures too — black and white, Asian and western.
Religious identities are less reliably obvious. I think of how
new these people are, how their names belong to a new world:
Seleka McManus, Chung Martinsson, Immaculata Weinstein,
Finlay Hanazaki, Makoto Galbraith. The last two are my
children but the others, if the internet is to be believed, are
theoretical people. They do not yet exist, but they will.

The families I follow in supermarkets are mostly in the
early stages of their revolt against identity. The children are
infants of four, five or six years old. Their parents have chosen,
or thoughtlessly fallen into a more difficult course. They will
not all stay together. Even so, I am optimistic. Their mere
existence persuades me that the source of something good is
still flowing, strengthening even, and that it can only be a
matter of time before it breaks down everything in its way.

On this occasion I am deep in the whitelands of central
Scotland and there is little to interest me. I get what I came
for and pay. I stand in the space between the checkouts and
the external wall of the building, now a curtain of blue-black
glass in the late afternoon, northern midwinter. It's cold

outside and rain has started to pearl the windows. I put the carrier bag between my feet to keep it upright – a penguin's egg of junk food and alcohol as I zip up my fleece and pull the collar around my neck before turning to leave. I look down the long aisle at a crowd as dense as any in the year. Multipacks of beer and salty snacks and hangover cures are being heaved into trolleys as the nation provisions itself for Hogmanay. Children plead their cases or slyly try to slip one more lurid and sugary item into the mountain of consumption in the hope that it will pass unnoticed. Some sit waiting on the seats provided, one absorbed in a pocket video game, trainer-shod feet dangling off the floor. A three-year-old takes a call on his mobile, a curved model in banana-yellow plastic.

This is journey's end for us, a victory celebration for the whole of history to date – all needs met and at a fair price too. The story that started with fishing for termites with a stick has finished here – a glaring, striplit hangar with sixty thousand product lines and twenty-four-hour opening. It used to be a mythical object we called cornucopia, but now it's real. After this, whatever remains of human history can be nothing more than detail and variation. Historians must promote their careers as best they can, but history isn't really ideas, it's hunger. When one ends, so does the other.

But I am not ordinarily given to philosophising in supermarkets. What made this visit so memorable? Most particularly it was the line of red plastic buckets at the end of each checkout – a line that stretched away into the distance and was reflected in the dark glass of the windows giving the effect, especially when the vision is a little blurred, of landing lights on a runway. They are there to collect money for the victims of the Asian tsunami. Collections for one good cause or another are common enough, but this is the only one I remember years later. The noise was different — a continual roll of percussion as handfuls of coins were dropped in without a single off-beat. A child, being held by his father, looks on the scene from the same tall vantage point as myself and insists on joining in. He is given some coins which he throws energetically into the red bucket. One clean new penny bounces out and rolls across the floor to where the three-year-old abandons his banana-phone call to pounce on its brightness and run across the aisle and stretch up on his toes to drop it back in.

It is late in the day and I wonder how long this has been going on. Have I chanced to look along this line at an unusually generous moment? Then I see, approaching from the far end, two members of the shop staff laboriously pushing a trolley bearing large plastic tubs. At every checkout they stop and empty the bucket of money into one of these larger containers, and it is clear that they must do this or else the buckets themselves would soon become too heavy to lift. At this rate it seems likely that they have to sweep the line every half-hour. For all I know they have been at it all day long. I head out, passing the last bucket in the line, checkout number one, noticing as I go that it contains not only coins, but many banknotes too.

It's blustery outside. Icy rain is strengthening and the temperature has fallen noticeably. I am parked in one of the last spaces, among the furthest from the store. I make my way there, hunched, defensive against one of those environments that best defines bleakness in modern life. When I get

to the car the chill has caused a mist to settle on the inside of the windows. I throw the bag on the back seat and slam the door shut. It is then that I notice something on the small fixed window, the one you could just reach if you were four or five years old and straining against the safety straps of your seat. It has been invisible until now, but has been brought out by the condensing cold like a photograph developing in a darkroom tray, or even by the moisture of a living breath. It is a circle drawn by a child's finger, two dots for eyes, a bent line for the nose and a broad upturned curve for the smile.

Woven through all this, and perhaps not too hard to tease out, there must be an answer to the question that started this chapter, to the question of what is left after the flood. It is the old answer, something about other people. It is the answer we all know, even if we live so much of our lives as if we had forgotten it.

Postscript

This a novelist's book. This means not only that its sources are the life and mind of the author but also that it has a certain swaggering disregard for scholarship. To equip it with the meticulous apparatus of notes and index could seem misleading, as well as being of little real use. Technology has rendered the footnote largely redundant and it is now an easy matter for a reader to follow my digital footsteps without the need for any old-fashioned ink and paper promptings from me. There are, nevertheless, some particular debts that must be acknowledged.

The story of Cristos Valenti in Chapter 2 is taken from Carol Delaney's *Abraham on Trial*, a wide-ranging cultural analysis of the Abraham and Isaac story. Delaney changed the names of those involved.

The Neil and McQuiston abduction cases in Chapter 4 come from *Kidnapped: Child Abduction in America*, by Paula S. Fass.

What little knowledge I have of Japan that is not derived from direct observation comes from several writers, Ian Buruma being the most useful of these. His books *The Wages of Guilt*, *The Japanese Mirror* and *Inventing Japan* are all accessible and economical in equal measure. Those who experience a mixture of puzzlement and regret at the ugliness of Japan's built environment will be helped by Alex Kerr's *Dogs and Demons: The Fall of Modern Japan*. On the postwar founding period of modern Japan — still very much there in spite of Kerr's title — John W. Dower's *Embracing Defeat* is the indispensable work. Needless to say, a Japanese guide is much to be preferred, and I can think of none that better combines insight and pleasure than the films of Yasujiro Ozu.

As for clear thinking about men and women, children and families, Brenda Almond's *The Fragmenting Family* offers the opportunity for a rigorous workout. Even those not always in sympathy with the author's views will benefit from the exercise of reading the book. In contrast to the present work, its detailed notes and bibliography are a useful signpost for those who wish to go further.

The names of Tomoko's sister and in-laws in Chapter 8 have been changed.

The author is grateful for permission to reproduce:

H. S. Wong, *Terrified baby, who was almost the only human being left alive, sitting nr. train tracks in South Station after brutal Japanese bombing during WWII* © H.S. Wong, Time & Life Pictures/Getty Images

World War II – Vienna 1945 © Yevgeny Khaldei/Agentur Voller Ernst/dpa/Corbis

E. V. Kealey, *Women of Britain Say – 'Go!' Recruitment Poster* © Swim Ink 2, LLC/CORBIS

Ultrasound scan of twenty-week-old foetus (B&W) © UHB Trust/Getty Images

Peter Steiner, 'On the Internet, nobody knows you're a dog.' © Peter Steiner/The New Yorker Collection/www.cartoonbank.com

Paula Modersohn-Becker, *Reclining Mother and Child II*, 1906 © Kunstsammlungen Böttcherstraße, Paula Modersohn-Becker Museum, Bremen

Artemisia Gentileschi, *Judith and Holofernes*, 1612–21 © The Bridgeman Art Library/Getty Images

Shanghai Station Bombed © Hulton-Deutsch Collection/CORBIS